The Chartered Facilities Manager

Copyright © 2020 Zulk Shamsuddin, PhD

GAFM ACADEMY

All rights reserved.

ISBN: 9798301353048

INTRODUCTION

The **Chartered Facilities Manager (ChFM)** is a world-class certification accredited by the Global Academy of Finance and Management ®. This credential is for individuals with skills and experience in facilities management, contract management, procurement management, project management, relationship management, risk and compliance, and ensuring that the facilities meet statutory requirements and comply with occupational health and safety standards.

It forms the basis of the assessment that individuals must pass to earn the Chartered Facilities Manager status and inclusion in the Directory of The GAFM Academy of Finance and Management Certified Professionals. Individuals with several years of experience in facilities management are encouraged to acquire this certification.

Differentiate yourself from the crowd with the Chartered Facilities Manager certification.

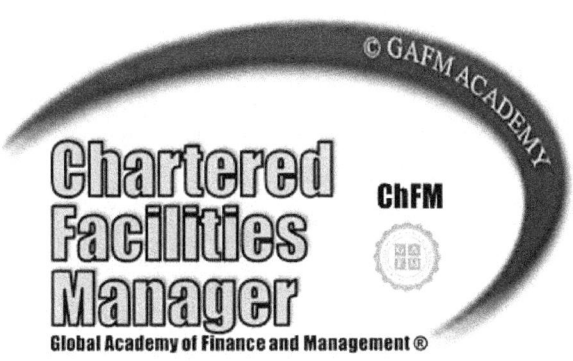

INTERNATIONAL BOARD OF STANDARDS CERTIFYING BODY

GAFM IBS International Board of Standards Certifying Body operate in over 40 nations worldwide and have members in over 150 countries. The IBS owns the certifications and trademarks conferred by the GAFM Global Academy of Finance and Management ® and The American Academy of Project Management ®. Our International Board of Standards Accreditation council is located in the EU and USA. Our Certification Body and Governance Team regulates the standards for certification and accredited education criteria for qualified training and degree programs which are a direct path to our certifications. The Board of Standards awards designations and board certification in the finance, accounting, risk, economics, and management consulting areas. The IBS is EU Accredited in Europe and ISO Certified for Quality and Training under ISO 21001 Standards. The IBS is a charter member signatory to the Higher Education Quality Standards Commission and a global standards agreement with the USA Accreditation agency ACBSP Accreditation Council for Business Schools and Programs and has been recognized on the AACSB website by the President. The IBS owns over 30 trademark certification brands and licenses the certifications to members around the world. Over 20 years of unmatched quality standards working with business schools worldwide.

Who should read this book?

Anyone with the required minimum qualifications and the necessary experience associated with facilities management should consider getting certified by reading this book.

IMPORTANCE OF CERTIFICATION

Certificates and certifications, the names for these credentials sound confusingly similar. But there are important differences. Here's what you need to know about these resume-enhancing options and how they might advance your career.

SKILLS AND QUALIFICATIONS

The facilities manager should be self-motivated, extremely organized, and have strong communication and project management aptitude. Employers typically seek candidates with a bachelor's degree and the following skills:

- Leadership and human relations skills
- Ability to quantify contributions to the productivity of the organization
- Ability to quantify the impact of various facility initiatives on the productivity of the employees and the organization
- Understanding the financial metrics of the organization

- Comprehending value to the end-user of the facility
- Communicating the strategic importance of facility management as a tool to support the organizational vision.
- Perceiving the knowledge economy in terms of meeting the needs of the facility's end-users
- Comprehending the use of technology for adding value
- Understanding the concept of branding a facility for the purposes of meeting the strategic needs of a facility's end-users

Benefits Of Becoming a Chartered Facilities Manager

- Understanding the processes associated with facilities management.
- Assess the knowledge and competencies of the processes associated with facilities management.
- Applying the appropriate techniques and tools for facilities management.
- Learn how facilities management fits into the overall enterprise facilities management
- Adopting best practices and methodology for the deployment of facilities management activities.

- Golden opportunity for Graduates and Professionals.
- Getting shortlist for a job opportunity.
- Applicants with a certified credential are usually the preferred choice among top recruiters and employers.
- Candidate with certification earn attractive compensation package comparatively with others with similar job.
- Recognized credibility.
- Greater employment prospects across the globe.
- Leveraging international quality accreditation (ISO Standards) to your name, and CV.
- Get recognition of your skills and competencies as specified on the accredited endorsement training certificate.
- Leveraging the certification card to establish professional relationship during social networking, corporate events, seminars, conferences, trainings, et cetera.
- Register your name in the GAFM® Directory of Certified or Chartered Professionals, share with future employers.

What is a Certification?

When you have the professional knowledge you need, a certification allows you to prove it. Certifications indicate mastery of skills or standards. Professional certifications are granted by industry groups or career-related organizations. These groups assess your qualifications, usually through an exam or application process. Many certifications include the privilege to use a related designation following your professional title. A professional certification differs from a license, which permits you to work in a certain profession and is usually issued by government or regulatory agencies.

Certification is about verifying your experience against a set of skills and competencies that are related to the specific job or role. Obviously you need to have the appropriate level of knowledge associated with the skills. You also need to have the minimum qualification (bachelor degree) and higher as a prerequisite for any certification.

KNOWLEDGE + QUALIFICATION + EXPERIENCE
are the cornerstones of GAFM® Certifications

Examination is not only based upon your knowledge, skills and competencies but also the methodologies, processes, and the industry standards that you need to know and practice in your past experience. At GAFM Academy, we provide an eBook to facilitate the examination process so that the assessments are aligned with the skills and competencies pertaining to the specific certification.

Skills and Competencies

This book addresses the following skills and competencies that you need to qualify for the Chartered Facilities Manager (ChFM) certification.

1. Facilities Management
2. Procurement Management
3. Contract Management
4. Project Management
5. Risk And Compliance
6. Relationship Management

Click the link below to apply for this certification

https://shorturl.at/cES36

FREQUENTLY ASKED QUESTIONS

Why do I need to submit a CV?

We only accept candidates who meet the minimum qualification requirements and credible work experience.

When will GAFM process my application?

Application will only be processed after payment is received.

How do I pay?

We accept payments via Credit / Debit card. Payment link will be shared once your application has been accepted.

Can I pay via bank wire transfer?

Yes, we will share the invoice with banking details.

How do I prepare myself for the exam?

This is a self-study model. An eBook will be provided, examination will be based on the information in the eBook. The eBook will be provided FREE to successful candidates after payment has been made.

How long is the duration of self-study period?

You must complete this study period inclusive of the exam within ten days from the date of payment.

How do I write the exam?

When you're ready to write the exam, kindly email us to book your schedule for the exam.

How do I apply for exemption from the exam?

This is at the discretion of the Board. You may be requested to submit additional information in addition to the CV submitted earlier. In any case, if your experience is good, we will apply for an exemption only after payment has been received.

How is the exam structured?

The examination comprised of 40 choice questions.

Difficulty: Moderate   Duration: 60 minutes

What is the passing grade?

70%

When will I know the result of the exam?

Within 48 hours

What if I failed in the first attempt?

You are allowed to rewrite the exam without any additional charge.

When will I receive the certification documents?

Shipping is within 10 business days after you complete the course.

What courier services do we use?

We ship via United Parcel Service / FedEx

What are the certification documents?

i) professional accredited certificate   ii) endorsement training certificate   iii) certification card

Can I get a digital copy of the certificates?

We do not issue digital copy.

What is the endorsement training certificate?

This is the certificate that indicate the skills and competencies associated with the professional accredited certificate where you have accomplished via the online training program.

Can I apply the designation after my name while waiting for the certification documents?

Yes

Certification will differentiate you from the crowd, from thousands of applications eyeing on that single job opening, your profile stands tall above the rest! You will be asking yourself – what makes you so special? How could a single piece of paper make a difference? What about the bachelor's degree certificate? Some of the candidates are better than you but why aren't they shortlisted?

You may think that since you have secured a job, getting certified is optional. Think again, this is 2024! When you are out of job for whatever reasons, retrenchment, corporate downsizing, economic downturn, office politics, et cetera then you start to feel the pressure to secure another job. Competition is intense out there, connections come handy but not everyone has strong cable these days. When you look at job adverts, although they did not explicitly mention that you must be certified to apply for the job opening, they do filter candidates based on these criteria when it comes to shortlist thousands of candidates.

So, you are left out of the opportunity to compete in the job marketplace! Then you start rushing to get certified. It's a little too late. By that time, the certification fee has gone up. If you do not have working experience then it is highly unlikely you will be offered to sit for any certification courses. This put fresh graduates in a highly difficult position. If you have the ambition to work abroad, you need to have at least one accredited and globally recognized certification to apply for jobs abroad being in the US, Europe, Middle East or elsewhere. If you don't have this, it is highly unlikely that you will get your application shortlisted.

Chapter 1 : FACILITIES MANAGEMENT

Facilities management strategy is a tool for facility management that focuses on improving the workplace to boost productivity, performance and well-being of workers in a company. For efficient and effective services, facilities management strategy allows the deeper understanding of the needs of an organization or business and places procedures and processes to meet these needs.

The right strategy goes beyond providing day to day support and service and starts creating long term initiatives that can sustain the life of assets and improve productivity. The driving force behind a facilities management strategy is the safety and happiness of the people in the facility.

WHAT IS FACILITY MANAGEMENT?

Facility management refers to how facilities at an organization are managed and maintained. These facilities are not limited to offices but can also include mechanical and electrical utilities or the company's physical resources with the potential to cause the employees a safety or health hazard. Facility management is affected by technology changes and advancements imploring facility managers to identify technology investments that can positively influence facilities management.

What Is A Facilities Management Strategy?

Facilities management strategy is a collaboration between facility management and facility planning focusing on long term outcomes and involves incorporating facility management into company initiatives. Facilities management strategy calls for an understanding of business goals and linking them to facility management to improve the workplace and organization. It's driven by goals.

Why Is Facility Management More Relevant Than Ever?

Facility management can ensure that companies are running efficiently and effectively. Buildings with a facility management team run properly as they are responsible for the daily analysis of utilities at the company as well as maintenance and repairs. They also take part in strategic planning activities of the company to aid the growth of employee productivity and cut down costs.

Studies have shown that the best workplace environment can affect productivity and improve the well-being of workers which can affect business output and the success of organizations as a whole. For example, clean working space and bathrooms can make workers feel comfortable and secure. Facilities management takes care of such services. With skilled management experts and your own facilities manager, we can offer you tailor-made management services both on a short or long-term basis so you can focus on other aspects of your business without worry.

FACILITY MANAGEMENT: Vacuuming the pool to remove debris that sits on the pool floor, as well as the walls and steps. Checking and cleaning the filter. Keeping the water circulating to help filter and prevent bacteria and algae growth. Checking the pool's chemical balance and pH levels.

WHAT ARE FACILITY MANAGEMENT'S OBJECTIVES?

Facility management involves so many responsibilities that include ensuring comfort, functionality, safety and happiness of occupants in a building that is being managed. To successfully accomplish all these, there are facility management objectives that should be met and these objectives can fit all types of facilities.

COMMUNICATION WITH STAKEHOLDERS AND OCCUPANTS

For everything to run smoothly as you manage a building, establish and maintain communication with occupants and stakeholders of the building. Such dialogue can help you learn how they view the facility and they can also offer invaluable suggestions to make the environment comfortable and safe.

PROVIDE A SAFE AND HEALTHY ENVIRONMENT

Safety is always our main concern in any organization. By being aware of potential health risks and creating strategies to correct and avoid some of these risks, the workplace can keep a lot of people safe. In managing building facilities, the bathrooms are an essential part of any building. By maintaining cleanliness, freshness and stocking them with adequate toiletries, we make them as pleasant as possible for every visit made. Facility management team also focuses on reducing the level of moisture and mold growth in bathrooms by doing regular inspections and investing in high-density polyethene that not only improves the quality of air but also prevents mold growth.

Be Mindful of Deficiencies

Some things if left unchecked for a long time can ultimately affect the functionality of utilities in a building. Routine checks can help identify any building deficiencies and avoid bigger problems in future. A facility manager is responsible to make these routine checks every three to 6 months.

Improve and Endorse Energy Efficiency

Making the facility more energy-efficient can save money. By going over the expenses of the building on water, gas and electricity a facility manager can identify how much is being spent and ways of reducing energy wastage. Investing in equipment that can save energy such as energy-efficient light bulbs, boosting existing equipment and sealing off leaks on pipes can reduce and prevent more wastage of energy.

What Are The 5 Steps in Strategic Facility Planning?

Strategic Facility Planning (SFP) is a key process that can enhance the delivery of services from a facility management team to its stakeholders. An SFP can reduce delays and customer dissatisfaction with services being offered and ensures that all facility management activities are in line with the corporate direction of the business. With SFP, a facility manager can help organizations become effective and conducive space for workers. The process follows these steps:

1) Clarify Your Strategic Position

To know the right needs of a facility, an analysis of the current position or conditions of the building must be done. The facility manager must study the values, culture, vision and goals of the organization they want to work with and develop strategies that will be in line with these core values. The facility manager must understand where the organization is heading, what changes might occur and how they will affect the real estate needs of the organization. This can help predict future needs, requirements and costs for operations, maintenance and space.

2) Prioritize Your Objectives

After identifying the needs, a facility manager must evaluate the objectives that collaborate with the core values and vision of the organization and how each chosen objective can help reach set goals. Priority should be given to objectives that are more urgent, relate more to the needs of stakeholders and can support the performance of everyone at the workplace.

3) Formulate A Strategy

Formulating a strategy involves identifying the right initiatives to reach set objectives and creating a time frame to reach them.

4) Implement and Manage the Strategy

With the plan on paper, it can be implemented, but for its success, everyone in the organization must be aware of what sort of strategies you have put in place. Facility management team members should know what their roles will be throughout the facility management plan.

5) Monitor and Evaluate Strategy

To determine if the strategy is successful, continue to monitor the work being done and check if progress matches up with set priorities. Facility managers can also take opinions from members of the organization to see if the work they are providing is up to their standards. Where priorities or changes must be made in approach, the facility manager is also responsible for these.

IMPLEMENTING STRATEGIC FM PLAN

It takes control to perfectly carry out strategic facility management. The International Facility Management Association list's four steps to successfully implement a strategic facility plan:

Understand

Strategic facility management plan is guided by goals and the capacity of facilities to support such goals. The strategy must be well understood before it is executed and this goes beyond knowing the time frame to identifying if the strategy has enough resources to run.

Analyze

The second step in developing strategic facility management plan calls for a deeper understanding and experimentation on how the plan can be put into action. Use experimental and analytic tools to help fully build the strategy. By using scenario planning you can have a systematic layout of the plan and to analyses focus areas we use SWOT (Strengths, Weaknesses, opportunities and Threats) analysis. Brainstorming and can help the whole team come up with facility improvement ideas.

Plan

Developing a strategic facility management plan is easy after outlining what you want to do and how to do it. A facility manager is usually the one who hands in this physical plan to executive managers for approval. The plan details what changes should be made to the facility, why they should happen and what needs to be done for such changes to occur. Like a business plan, the facility management plan shows the time frame for actions, responsibilities of team members and shows how success will be measured.

Act

After the facility management plan is approved, it's time for action. Strategic facility management requires leaders that can execute the changes in line with the strategic management facilities plan and who are able to track and report changes and improvements to the overall plan. These leaders should value the vision at the facilities level and know how it affects the goals of the business. After implementation, continue to measure the success of the strategy on different aspects of the business.

BUSINESS CONTINUITY PLANNING

Some facilities depend on fully functioning equipment to run. A business continuity plan (BCP) is like a contingency plan that identifies the key assets of a facility and the potential risks that the asset has. The plan also shows how business operations could be affected if the asset stopped functioning. With evaluation and the right plan, you can ensure that a business or facility does not stop its operations if the inevitable should occur.

Facilities management is the process by which an organization ensures that its buildings, systems, and services support the organization's core operations and processes as well as contribute to achieving its strategic objectives in changing conditions. It focuses resources on meeting user needs to support the key role of people in organizations and strives to continuously improve quality, reduce risks and ensure value for money. It is an important management function and business service. Major organizations worldwide are using it as part of their strategy for restructuring to provide a competitive edge. It can also ensure that buildings and support services improve customer responsiveness and contribute to business objectives.

The scope of the facilities management services covers all aspects of property, space, environmental control, health and safety, and support services, and requires that appropriate control points are established in the organization. The facilities management plan will set out these policies and identify corporate guidelines and standards. It will describe the organization, its structure, procedures and responsibilities. Facilities management policies lay out an organization's response to vital issues such as space allocation and charging, environmental control and protection, and direct and contract employment. The policies will set a direction for the organization and establish the values of and attitudes toward the facilities users including the corporation, its operating units and customers, individual employees and the public.

Facilities management entails the integration of people, technology and support services to achieve an organization's mission. It is concerned primarily with the quality of service to all stakeholders in the organization. In a service level model, the informed buyer assesses needs, agrees on the desired service levels and purchases services to meet them. The facilities organization must enable managers to focus on buying the best standard of service achievable within an agreed budget.

The primary objective of facility management is to deliver the optimum facility management services stipulated in the contractual agreement within the scope, budget, and quality requirements. The emphasis here is on management and business rather than the technical aspects of the facility management mission.

Both the organization and the facility manager should have a specific philosophy about facilities.

- Facility management is an essential business function; the facility manager is a business manager and should be placed at the same level as the managers of human relations and/or information technology.
- Different types of organizations require different approaches to facility management (and services may be provided in-house or contracted out), but there are a limited number of ways to organize depending upon the mission.
- Every FM organization will have some element contracted out so contract negotiation and administration skills are essential for every facility manager.
- Facility managers need to be innovative in their contracting. Low-bid contracts are seldom appropriate, and we must partner with our contractors and consultants while insisting that they perform if they are to continue working for us.
- Good facility management is based on the good leadership of a proper organization.
- Facility managers need to have the same level of business skills as their management colleagues.
- Facility managers must know their business both the FM business and the business they support.
- While it is improving, facility management needs better basic research and better application of both existing research and best practices.
- Facility managers are in a position where they can influence how substantial organizational resources are spent. Conduct your business with the highest degree of ethics and a sense of stewardship.

- Sustainability, security, and emergency management are functions with great management and customer interest, which every FM must accommodate.

THE FACILITIES MANAGEMENT TEAM

A major challenge for the facility manager is forming a facility's staff and getting it to function as a team. Unfortunately, many factors in a company work counter to a team approach, which is why a facility manager must be a leader, not simply a manager. We have mentioned repeatedly the diverse nature of staffing in most facility departments; staff, contractors, and consultants. This allows for both maximizations of skills and flexibility to meet peak workloads. Yet all members of the team, regardless of employment status, must feel that they are important members of one team. This is true even for one-time contractors. In some organizations, even though it makes sense, a staff member is never to be placed in a position subordinate to a consultant. Bureaucratic personnel policies or traditions that preclude such assignments often run contrary to effective team building and require an aggressive leader to get them modified. In today's contractor and consultant-laden business world, this consultant may be the best (or only) person, to train, manage, and guide an employee, regardless of staffing status.

Unfortunately, some good management techniques often run contrary to good teamwork. Excessive dependence on quantitative measurement, particularly measuring one work unit against another, often leads to cutting corners, bickering, and even sabotage. Quantitative measurements always must be evaluated in context and used as indicators for discussion on ways to improve, not as the final word. Likewise, subordinate objectives must reinforce departmental goals. Successful teamwork and subordinates who stress an understanding and support of the entire organization must be rewarded.

Quality Service Management

The main principle of service management is to ensure the facilities management (FM) project will meet or exceed stakeholders' needs and expectations. The FM project team must develop a good relationship with key stakeholders, especially the project sponsor and the key project stakeholders of the project, to understand what quality means to them. One of the causes for poor project evaluations is the project focuses only on meeting the written requirements for the main outputs and ignores other stakeholder needs and expectations for the project.

Quality must be viewed on an equal level with scope, schedule, and budget. If a project sponsor is not satisfied with the quality of how the project is delivering the outcomes, the project team will need to make adjustments to the scope, schedule, and budget to satisfy the project sponsor's needs and expectations. To deliver the project scope on time and within budget is not enough. To achieve stakeholder satisfaction the project must develop a good working relationship with all stakeholders and understand their stated or implied needs.

Quality Service Management consists of three main processes.

Plan Quality Management

Plan Quality Management refers to the process of identifying quality requirements and standards for the project and its deliverables and documenting how the project will demonstrate compliance with quality requirements.

Perform Quality Assurance

Perform Quality Assurance refers to the process of auditing the quality requirements and the results from quality control measurements to ensure that appropriate quality standards and operational definitions are used.

Control Quality

Control Quality refers to the process of monitoring and recording results of executing quality activities to assess performance and recommend necessary changes.

QUALITY MANAGEMENT PLANNING

The first step in the quality management planning process is to define the quality objectives of the FM services. The facilities manager and the team must identify what quality standards will be used in the project, it will look at the project sponsor, key project stakeholders, the organization and other project stakeholders to come up with a good definition of quality. In some instances, the organization or the area of specialization of the project (engineering, information technology, FM, health, water, or education) may have some standard definitions of quality that can be used by the FM project.

Identifying quality standards is a key component of quality definition that will help identify the key characteristics that will govern FM project activities and ensure the key project stakeholders and project sponsors will accept the project outcomes.

Quality management implies the ability to anticipate situations and prepare actions that will help bring the desired outcomes. The goal is the prevention of defects through the creation of actions that will ensure that the project team understands what is defined as quality.

SOURCES OF QUALITY DEFINITION

One source for the definition of quality comes from the project sponsor. the project must establish conversations with the project sponsor to be familiar with and come to a common understanding of what the project sponsor defines as quality. The project sponsor may have certain standards of what is expected from the project, and how the project delivers the expected benefits to the key project stakeholders. This is in line with the project's ultimate objective that the project outcomes have the ability to satisfy the stated or implied needs.

Another source for quality definition comes from the key project stakeholders; the project team must be able to understand how the key project stakeholders define quality from their perspective, a perspective that is more focused on fitness for use, the project outcomes must be relevant to the current needs of the key project stakeholders and must result in improvements to their lives. The team can create, as part of the baseline data collection, questions that seek to understand how the key project stakeholders define the project will meet their needs and a question that also helps define what project success looks like from the perspective of a beneficiary.

The development organization may have its own quality standards that can reflect the technical and managerial nature of the project. The organization may require from the project timely and accurate delivery of project information needed for decision-making, or compliance to international or locally recognized quality standards that define specific technical areas of the project, this is quite often in health, water and nutrition projects.

QUALITY CHARACTERISTICS

All materials or services have characteristics that facilitate the identification of its quality. The characteristics are part of the conditions of how the material, equipment and services are able to meet the requirements of the project and are fit for use by the key project stakeholders. Quality characteristics relate to the attributes, measures and methods attached to that particular product or service.

Functionality

is the degree, by which equipment performs its intended function, this is important, especially for clinical equipment, that the operation should behave as expected.

Performance

is how well a product or service performs the key project stakeholders intended use. A water system should be designed to support extreme conditions and require little maintenance to reduce the cost to the community and increase its sustainability.

Reliability

represents the ability of the service or product to perform as intended under normal conditions without unacceptable failures. The material used for blood testing should be able to provide the information consistently and dependably that will help identify critical diseases. The trust of the key project stakeholders is dependent upon the quality of the tests.

Relevance

represents the characteristic of how a product or service meets the actual needs of the key project stakeholders, it should be pertinent, applicable, and appropriate to its intended use or application.

Timeliness

represents how the product or service is delivered in time to solve the problems when its needed and not after, this is a crucial characteristic for health and emergency relief work.

Suitability

defines the fitness of its use, its appropriateness and correctness, the agriculture equipment must be designed to operate on the sole condition the key project stakeholders will use it on.

Completeness

defines the quality that the service is to be completed and includes the entire scope of services. Training sessions should be completed and include all the material needed to build a desired skill or knowledge.

Consistency

ensures services are delivered in the same way for every beneficiary. For example, clinical tests need to be done using the same procedure for every patient.

Does the product or service meet its intended purpose?

Machine is useless if the suction module failed to function

Quality characteristics are not limited to the material, equipment or service delivered to the key project stakeholders, but also apply to the material, equipment, and services the project staff uses to deliver the project outputs. These include the vehicles, computers, various equipment, tools and consulting services the project purchases and uses to carry out its activities.

Quality characteristics must be included in all materials, equipment and services the project will purchase, the procurement officers must have a complete description of what is required by the project, otherwise, a procurement office may purchase the goods or services based on her or his information of the product.

What went wrong - A project requested the purchase of 1000 tents for a community displaced by floods, the purchase request had no specifications for its intended use (suitability), and resistance (performance). The procurement officer only knew that the tents were needed as soon as possible (timeliness), so he purchased, based on his knowledge of what a tent looks like, 1000 camping tents, they were delivered to the refugee camps on the requested timeframe, and the project manager was happy. But the next day all families that received the tents were complaining that they were not good for the cold nights and too small to accommodate their extended families. The project purchased the tents under budget and within the specified timeframe but the key project stakeholders rejected them because they did not meet their needs (quality services are poor).

Quality Management Plan

A FM Quality Management Plan is a document, or several documents, that together specify quality standards, practices, resources, specifications, and the sequence of activities relevant to a particular product, service, project, or contract.

FM Quality Management Plan define:

- Objectives to be attained (for example, characteristics or specifications, uniformity, effectiveness, aesthetics, cycle time, cost, natural resources, utilization, yield, dependability, and so on).
- Steps in the processes that constitute the operating practice or procedures of the organization.
- Allocation of responsibilities, authority, and resources during the different phases of the process or project.
- Specific documented standards, practices, procedures, and instructions to be applied.
- Suitable testing, inspection, examination, and audit programs at appropriate stages.
- A documented procedure for changes and modifications to a quality plan as a process is improved.
- A method for measuring the achievement of quality objectives.
- Other actions necessary to meet the objectives.

At the highest level, quality goals and plans should be integrated with the overall strategic plans of the organization. As organizational objectives and plans are deployed throughout the organization, each function fashions its own best way of contributing to the top-level goals and objectives.

At lower levels, the quality plan assumes the role of an actionable plan. Such plans may take many different forms depending on the outcome they are to produce. Quality plans may also be represented by more than one type of document to produce a given outcome.

Part of defining quality involves developing a quality management plan and a quality checklist that will be used during the project implementation phase. This checklist will ensure the project team and other actors are delivering the project outputs according to the quality requirements.

Once the project has defined the quality standards and quality characteristics, it will create a project quality plan that describes all the quality definitions and standards relevant to the project, it will highlight the standards that must be followed to comply to regulatory requirements set up by the project sponsor, the organization and external agencies such as the local government and professional organizations (health, nutrition, etc.)

The quality plan also describes the conditions that the services and materials must possess in order to satisfy the needs and expectations of the project stakeholders, it describes the situations or conditions that make an output fall below quality standards, this information is used to gain a common understanding among the project team to help them identify what is above and what is below a quality standard.

The quality plan also includes the procedure to ensure that the quality standards are being followed by all project staff. The plan also includes the steps required to monitor and control quality and the approval process to make changes to the quality standards and the quality plan.

EXAMPLE OF A QUALITY MANAGEMENT PLAN

Let's take a look at a manufacturing company that machines metal parts. Its quality plan consists of applicable procedures that includes describing the production process and responsibilities, applicable workmanship standards, the measurement tolerances acceptable, the description of the material standards, and so forth. These may all be separate documents.

More variable information that pertains to a particular customer may be spelled out on individual work orders. Work orders specify the machine setups and tolerances, operations to be performed, tests, inspections, handling, storing, packaging, and delivery steps to be followed.

An operating-level quality plan translates the customer requirements into actions required to produce the desired outcome and couples this with applicable procedures, standards, practices, and protocols to specify precisely what is needed, who will do it, and how it will be done. A quality control plan may specify product tolerances, testing parameters, and acceptance criteria. While the terminology may differ, the basic approach is similar for service and other types of organizations.

QUALITY ASSURANCE

Assurance is the activity of providing evidence to create confidence among all stakeholders that the quality-related activities are being performed effectively; and that all planned actions are being done to provide adequate confidence that a product or service will satisfy the stated requirements for quality.

Quality Assurance (QA) is a process to provide confirmation based on evidence to ensure to the project sponsor, key project stakeholders, organization management and other stakeholders that product meet needs, expectations, and other requirements. It assures the existence and effectiveness of process and procedures tools, and safeguards are in place to make sure that the expected levels of quality will be reached to produce quality outputs.

Quality Assurance occurs during the implementation phase of the project and includes the evaluation of the overall performance of the project on a regular basis to provide confidence that the project will satisfy the quality standards defined by the project.

Does the product or service conform to the requirements?

One of the purposes of quality management is to find errors and defects as early in the project as possible. Therefore, a good quality management process will end up taking more effort hours and cost upfront. The goal is to reduce the chances that products or services will be of poor quality after the project has been completed.

QA is done not only to the products and services delivered by the project but also to the process and procedures used to manage the project, that includes the way the project uses the tools, techniques and methodologies to manage scope, schedule, budget and quality. Quality assurance also includes the project meets any legal or regulatory standards.

How will risks impact a project QUALITY?

Quality will be severely impacted because the project failed to produce the deliverables within scope, schedule, and budget.

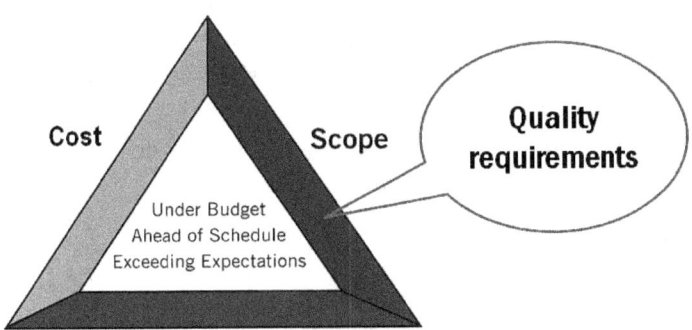

PROJECT BUDGET MUST INCLUDE A QUALITY ASSURANCE FUNCTION

The simple fact is that quality is an indispensable part of any effort. Delivering FM services without quality controls is wrought with risk: it will not satisfy your customer, and will reflect poorly on your reputation. Assuming that you cannot do a change control to add a quality assurance (QA) function to your FM project budget, the good news is that, in a pinch, you can do without a separate QA function by incorporating quality assurance into every procedure and task, and taking on quality control responsibilities yourself.

QUALITY AUDIT

Quality audits are structured reviews of the FM quality management activities that help identify lessons learned that can improve the performance of current or future FM services. Audits are performed by project staff or FM consultants with expertise in specific areas. The purpose of a quality audit is to review how the project is using its internal processes to produce the services it will deliver to the key project stakeholders. Its goal is to find ways to improve the tools, techniques and processes that create the FM services. If problems are detected during the quality audits, corrective action will be necessary to the tools, processes and procedures used to ensure quality is re-established. Part of the audit may include a review of the project staff understanding of the quality parameters or metrics, and the skills expertise and knowledge of the people in charge of producing or delivering the products or services. If corrective actions are needed, these must be approved through the change control processes.

QUALITY MANAGEMENT VS QUALITY AUDIT

- Quality Management is all the activities that are intended to bring about the desired level of quality.

- Quality Audit is the procedural control that ensure participants are adequately following the required procedures.

- These concepts are related, but should not be confused. In particular, Quality Audit relates to the approach to quality that is laid down in quality standards such as the ISO-900x standards.

THE PDCA CYCLE

The most popular tool used to determine quality assurance is the Shewhart Cycle. This cycle for quality assurance consists of four steps: Plan, Do, Check, and Act. These steps are commonly abbreviated as PDCA.

The four quality assurance steps within the PDCA model stand for:

- **Plan:** Establish objectives and processes required to deliver the desired results.

- **Do**: Implement the process developed.
- **Check**: Monitor and evaluate the implemented process by testing the results against the predetermined objectives
- **Act**: Apply actions necessary for improvement if the results require changes.

The PDCA is an effective method for monitoring quality assurance because it analyzes existing conditions and methods used to provide the product or service to key project stakeholders. The goal is to ensure that excellence is inherent in every component of the process. Quality assurance also helps determine whether the steps used to provide the product or service is appropriate for the time and conditions. In addition, if the PDCA cycle is repeated throughout the lifetime of the project helping improve internal efficiency.

Quality assurance demands a degree of detail in order to be fully implemented at every step. Planning, for example, could include an investigation into the quality of the raw materials used in manufacturing, the actual assembly, or the inspection processes used. The Checking step could include beneficiary feedback or surveys to determine if beneficiary needs are being met or exceeded and why they are or are not. Acting could mean a total revision in the delivery process in order to correct a technical flaw. The goal to exceed stakeholder expectations in a measurable and accountable process is provided by quality assurance.

ASSURANCE VS. CONTROL

Quality assurance is often confused with quality control; quality control is done at the end of a process or activity to verify that quality standards have been met. Quality control by itself does not provide quality, although it may identify problems and suggest ways to improve it. In contrast, quality assurance is a systematic approach to obtaining quality standards.

Quality assurance is something that must be planned for from the earliest stages of a project, with appropriate measures taken at every stage. Unfortunately, far too many development projects are implemented with no quality assurance plan, and these projects often fail to meet the quality expectations of the project sponsor and key project stakeholders. To avoid problems the project must be able to demonstrate consistent compliance with the quality requirements for the project.

BUILDING REGULATIONS AND FIRE SAFETY COMPLIANCE

Performance-based fire safety provisions look at the outcomes of a successful system for fire minimization and control in a workplace or organization, without describing the detail of how this is to be achieved. For example, in Australia the Building Code has a series of performance requirements for the structural elements of a building, one of which is the FRL or fire-resistance level. This has up to three parts: structural adequacy; integrity; and insulation (in that order). Each is expressed in terms of minutes of required satisfactory performance; e.g. an FRL of 240/240/240 means that the structural elements would perform for four hours on all three criteria. There are performance requirements for, for example, fire doors, fire shutters and fire-stopping material (material for plugging 'penetrations' in floors, etc.). On the other hand, an example of prescriptive requirements is that for penetration of a floor, wall or ceiling by a cable or cluster of wires. This requires penetrations to have a specified maximum cross-section.

LEGAL REQUIREMENTS FOR FIRE SAFETY

Specific reference to fire safety is not generally included in the actual OHS act, but there will be reference to fire safety in most of the accompanying regulations. The regulations vary in adequacy.

BUILDING REGULATIONS AND MINIMUM STANDARDS OF FIRE SAFETY

Obviously, building design alone can only be partly successful in preventing fire. Other important factors are:

- good housekeeping, separation and segregation of materials and proper storage, e.g. fire cabinets for solvents
- the transport and handling of flammable materials
- the behavior of personnel, e.g., smoking, disposal of paper, cigarettes and matches
- adhering only to uses for which the building was designed, e.g. no solvent-based printing if not designed for that
- selection of wall and floor coverings and furniture which will not spread flame from an ignition source, and will minimize the speed of travel
- extreme care with radiant heaters, and preferably use of tilt-switched radiant heaters, or wall-mounted radiant heaters
- great care with high temperature sources used in maintenance such as welding equipment
- electrical design, installation, repair and maintenance to meet national or accepted standards.

The approach to fire in buildings falls into two key areas:

- design to prevent fire
- design to limit the spread of a fire if it starts, and to limit the effects of that fire.

Before building any new buildings, an application for approval must generally be submitted to the appropriate level of government. Fire design of buildings is based on the observed characteristics of fires, some of which have been carefully reproduced in places such as the UK Fire Research Station.

These characteristics are:

- in most cases the fire will only develop if there is fuel above the initial ignition source
- combustible materials in the path of the flames increase the size and intensity of the fire
- hot gases and flames, as they are lighter than air, travel upwards
- fire tends to follow vertical paths of travel – i.e. chimneys, flues, stairways, and the interior of stud walls – but drafts or forced airflows, e.g. in underground mines, can change this characteristic
- ceilings can be a barrier to this upward spread
- sometimes the lateral and downward spread is increased by the presence of highly flammable coatings or bonding, glues, varnishes and lacquers
- the likelihood of flammable surfaces catching fire from radiant heat energy, rather than direct spread, depends to some extent on the rate of burning of the fire in materials providing the radiant heat.

WORKPLACE FIRE SAFETY TIPS

Fires are among the biggest cause of casualties in the workplace, but being proactive and implementing a fire plan can significantly help reduce the risk. The most important thing to consider when creating a fire plan is to determine the likelihood of a fire.

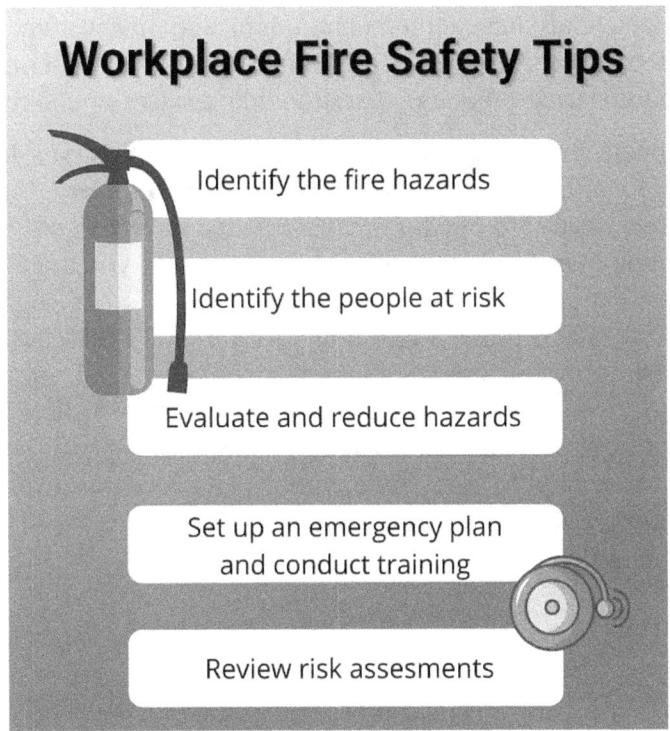

IDENTIFY THE RISKS

A fire hazard may look different in each workplace. From the fire triangle, we know that the 3 sources of fire are ignition, fuel and oxygen. Identify areas that carry the risk of ignition such as electrical equipment, boilers, hot works processes, steam pipes, and other sources of heat.

Define the classification of fuels in your workplace and the type of fire extinguisher required. Class A fuels include wood, paper, cloth, trash, plastics, or any solid combustible materials that are not metals. Class B fuels are flammable liquids like gasoline, oil, grease, acetone, or any non-metal in a liquid state, on fire. Class C fuels are energized electrical equipment so, as long as it's "plugged in," it would be considered a class C fire. Class D fuels are metals, potassium, sodium, aluminum, and magnesium. Lastly, Class K fuels are defined as a cooking fire involving combustion from liquids used in food preparation, like greases or cooking oils.

And of course, fires only need about 16% of oxygen to burn. Trying to minimize oxygen flow in fires across large areas or plants isn't feasible but for small fires, using dirt, sand, or non-flammable blankets is recommended. Make sure you are aware of any ventilation, air conditioning systems, or other sources of airflow in hazard-prone areas. If there's a fire, of course, everyone is at risk. But it's critical to know who is in and around the premises, who among your staff work alone or in isolated areas, requires extra care such as elders or workers with special needs, or is new to the facility. Keeping continuous track of this information will simplify your evacuation plan and processes in the case of an emergency.

EVALUATE AND REDUCE RISKS

Removing fire hazards in the workplace is easier said than done, but preventative action can be taken. Make sure not to use any damaged electrical cords or tools and to not overload circuits. Equipment maintenance and safe chemical usage and storage are also important factors in preventing fire hazards. Keeping your work area clean from dust and debris may sound like basic housekeeping, but as we can see from the Imperial Sugar Company dust explosion, keeping dust from building up in the workplace can be a matter of life and death.

Use PPE when in contact with fire hazards such as but not limited to flame-resistant gloves, jackets, and pants. OSHA states that if fire hazards are present, or likely to be present in the workplace the employer will have each affected employee use the types of PPE that will protect the affected employee from the hazards identified in the hazard assessment.

So, what does an emergency plan look like?

- Have a preferred method for reporting fires and other emergencies.
- Make sure evacuation policy and procedures are in place.
- Determine route assignments, such as floor plans, workplace maps, and safe or refuge areas.
- Keep all names, titles, departments, and telephone numbers of individuals both within and outside your company to contact for additional information or explanation of duties and responsibilities under the emergency plan;
- Create procedures for employees who remain to shut down or perform critical plant operations, operate fire extinguishers, or perform other essential services that cannot be shut down for every emergency alarm before evacuating; and
- Establish rescue and medical duties for any workers designated to perform them.

If your workplace is required to have an emergency plan, the employer is then required to provide the necessary training regarding workplace fire safety. Basic training for employers, employees, management, or engineers includes hazard communication, handling of materials, fire detection and prevention requirements, fire extinguishers, and more. Conducting periodic evacuation drills and fire extinguisher inspections can also help reinforce the steps and actions that need to be taken across your workforce.

BUILDING COMPLIANCE WITH FIRE SAFETY REGULATIONS

Building codes may include:
- fire-resisting construction
- compartmentation and separation

- protection of openings
- structural tests for lightweight construction
- early fire hazard indices
- fire doors, smoke doors, fire windows and shutters
- penetrations
- emergency lighting, exit signs and warning systems
- smoke hazard management
- fire-fighting equipment, and when sprinklers are required
- lift installations
- fire isolated exits
- number of exits
- distances to exits and second exits.

FIRE-RESISTING CONSTRUCTION (FIRE RESISTANCE AND STABILITY)

This includes constructing a building to protect it from fire in another, and using materials which minimize the spread of fire and generation of smoke and toxic gases. 'Stability' must be enough to allow escape and firefighter safety, and to minimize collapse onto nearby property. Standard fire tests are used to decide if different parts of a building will perform satisfactorily. 'Structural adequacy' looks at the ability of a structural part to continue to support a load. The 'integrity' aspect looks at how well a structural member prevents fire, gases and flames getting through it. Insulation is designed to limit heat transmission so that something on the other side of a wall or floor does not receive enough heat flow to ignite.

Compartmentation And Separation

Compartmentation refers to the division of a building into 'compartments' separated by structural material of specified fire resistance, such as a fire wall, to prevent spread of fire and smoke, and facilitate access by firefighters. 'Separation' limits the opportunity for the fire to spread to other buildings. (There was recently a fatal blaze in a park home (semiportable home) which threatened to ignite others nearby.) It also refers to separation of certain key equipment such as sprinkler valve equipment. Separation for dangerous goods also separates the goods from fire sources such as roadways.

Protection Of Openings

Certain types and layouts of doorways, windows, infill panels and fixed or openable glazed areas may be covered by a building code. It may include, for example, distances between windows on either side of a fire wall, and where protection of the opening is required, internal or external wall-wetting sprinklers, or automatic fire doors for doorways, automatic fire shutters for windows or construction of approved FRL for other openings.

Structural Tests For Lightweight Construction

These may cover the requirements for materials such as sheet or board, plaster, sprayed insulation, and concrete mixed with soft products such as pumice, which can be damaged by impact, pressure or abrasion, and thinner forms of masonry.

Early Fire Hazard Indices

These deal with materials, linings and surface finishes in buildings, particularly fire-isolated exits. Three indices are used flammability, spread-of-flame and smoke developed, which are measured by standard tests. In addition, protection of sides and edges from exposure to air may be a requirement.

Fire Doors, Smoke Doors, Fire Windows And Shutters

Fire doors are required to meet certain specifications and glazed parts must meet the integrity requirement in the FRL. Smoke doors must of course prevent smoke passing and, if glazed, minimize the risk of injury if a person accidentally walks into them.

Penetrations

Penetrations refer to services which penetrate walls, floors and ceilings required to have a FRL. Metal and UPVC pipes, wires and cables, electrical switches and outlets, and the fire-stopping material are all considered.

Emergency Lighting, Exit Signs, And Warning Systems

This part of a building code may cover the requirements for provision and design of lighting and emergency signage which will retain illumination in occupied areas and in egress ways, such as fire-isolated stairways, ramps or passageways independent of the normal power supply.

Smoke Hazard Management

Various classifications of buildings may be required by a code to have smoke control systems. This includes particular requirements such as natural smoke venting, smoke exhaust systems, air handling systems of a particular design, and smoke doors. In particular, smoke must be excluded from fire-isolated exits.

Lift Installations

A number of issues arise with lifts. These include restrictions on use in a fire, fitting out as an emergency lift for mobility-challenged people and fire service personnel, and prevention of spread-of-fire by way of lift shafts and doors.

Fire-Isolated Exits

Fire-isolated exits, and the provision for reaching them via fire-isolated stairways and ramps, are important features in some buildings.

Distances To Exits And Second Exits

The distance to an exit is clearly an important issue. Requirements vary with the class of building.

Fire-Fighting Equipment And When Sprinklers Are Required

Fire-fighting equipment includes fire hydrants, hose reels, sprinklers and fire control centers. Special care is needed in a building being constructed, in which sources of ignition may be more likely and fire systems are yet to be installed.

Fire Extinguishers

While many fire authorities require the installation of fire extinguishers in laboratories, the CHO should understand that, because of the relatively high nozzle pressure of extinguishers, the stream of the released extinguishing materials may sweep many breakable chemical containers off laboratory benches or cabinets and thereby contribute to explosive and flammable risk, as well as to the risk of toxic fumes generated either through heat or the reactivity of mixed chemicals. Extinguishers should be used in the laboratory only by authorized personnel who have received appropriate training, which should include actual practice. In the absence of an ongoing commitment to such training, the CHO is advised that it is best to focus on laboratory evacuation and to restrict the use of extinguishers to fight so-called "basket-fires" (i.e., fires that can easily be extinguished with minimal involvement of the overall laboratory space). Of course, the selection of extinguishing materials, including those contained in portable extinguishers or in any automatic fire suppressant system, must be guided by the reactivity (e.g., water reactivity) of laboratory chemicals, and should be undertaken only in strict coordination with fire science professionals.

DESIGN FEATURES OF A BUILDING AFFECTING STRUCTURAL INTEGRITY

TYPE OF CONSTRUCTION

As mentioned earlier the particular method of construction of a building, and its layout, affect its structural integrity in a fire. For a building of multiple classification, the most fire-resisting type of construction may be required, applying the most classification for a single floor to all floors, with perhaps certain exceptions. Sports spectator venues need special attention. A soccer ground fire at the Bradford Football Stadium in the United Kingdom in 1985 indicates how important this is.

COMPARTMENTATION AND SEPARATION

Compartmentation and separation affect the spread of fire and smoke, and codes may cover maximum sizes of fire compartments and atria. Atria (atriums) in buildings potentially could allow easy travel of fire and smoke from level to level.

VERTICAL SEPARATION AND FIRE WALLS

Vertical separation of openings such as windows is generally covered in codes, and fire walls which create compartment. (In a recent two-floor school fire, the fire spread rapidly along the ceiling because fire walls did not break up the ceiling space.)

LIFT (ELEVATOR) SHAFTS, SPRINKLER VALVES AND OPENINGS

Lift shafts could easily transmit fire and smoke and these are covered in codes. Certain equipment such as sprinkler valves must be fire-isolated. Openings in external walls and fire walls require protection.

SERVICES AND PENETRATIONS

Services passing through a floor are covered by codes. Penetrations of floors, walls or ceilings between compartments for cables, etc., have a limit on size and must be fire-stopped, e.g. caulked with suitable material. Materials, linings and surface finishes are covered, and may deal with what are called 'early fire hazard indices', EFHIs.

SPRINKLERS

Codes generally set out sprinkler requirements.

METHODS OF IMPROVING FIRE SAFETY OF BUILDINGS

'Passive protection' refers to protecting a building by attempting to confine a fire to the area in which it started. Automatic venting or blocking of the products of combustion is involved.

Passive protection includes:
- fire-retarding treatments and material

- air conditioning which can switch to fire mode, i.e. no return air recycling
- stairway, passageway and lift shaft pressurization if a fire occurs
- the correct fire rating of all walls, roofs, doors, floors, ceilings, windows and structural members
- fire doors, fire windows and fire shutters.

Smoke and heat management is important to allow occupants to escape and to reduce the temperature build-up. 'Active protection' is aimed at detecting and extinguishing a fire once it has started. It includes:

- fire and smoke detectors and alarms
- fire hydrants, hose reels and extinguishers, including water pressure booster pumps
- automatic sprinkler systems
- gas flooding systems
- evacuation systems.

The detection system can be wired to a fire panel and also linked to the fire services.

REQUIREMENTS FOR EGRESS FROM A BUILDING

Building codes cover access and egress, and emergency lighting, exit signs and warning systems. It may involve fire-isolated passageways, ramps and stairways. An 'exit' has a wide range of meanings; generally, it takes the form of an internal or external stairway, a doorway opening to a street or open space, a fire-isolated passageway or a doorway situated within a fire wall. The door has to open in the direction of travel to the outside. The best building design in the world is no use if the exit is locked or blocked with goods. Exit doors must be readily openable while the building is occupied. Exit doors must not be chained, bolted, fastened, or obstructed in any way. They should be openable by a single-handed action from the inside by a single device. They must not be blocked by traffic or parked vehicles on the outside. Special attention is required for invalids, people in bed due to illness, elderly people, people whose movement is impaired, very young children, and people in captivity.

BUILDING DESIGN, EMERGENCY PROCEDURES AND HUMAN BEHAVIOR

In situations where people have died in a fire, generally it is smoke and toxic gas inhalation which kills or renders people unconscious so they cannot escape rather than heat itself. While it is necessary to sound an alarm and alert people so that they respond ('Fire!'), there is the risk that panic can arise. This is more likely if there is a delay in giving a warning, and hence time is short to evacuate a large number of people. If exits to the outside are blocked or have been locked, and a crush develops, people can panic further. In some cases, such as the Bradford soccer stadium fire in the UK, many people died from crushing, not from fire. (Multiple deaths also resulted from exits with illegal locking or from inadequate egress in the Whisky A Go Go nightclub fire in Brisbane, the Stardust nightclub fire in Dublin and a more recent nightclub fire in Shanghai.) A prompt and clear response by well-trained staff will ensure that panic is minimized and evacuation is effective. It is important that physically challenged people are properly briefed in advance, because if they set off down an emergency stair at the wrong time they can obstruct the exit of many others. Problems can arise in buildings where large numbers of people inside are casual visitors, such as in major shopping centers. Tenants may change and appointment of new wardens overlooked. Exit routes should be well marked and signposting good. Panic can cause people to overlook obvious escape routes, and can lead to individual competitive responses rather than orderly behavior where members of a group look after each other.

BENCHMARKING FACILITIES COSTS

In facilities management, benchmarking has been defined as 'a process of comparing a product, service process, indeed, any activity or object, with other samples from a peer group, with a view to identifying 'best buy' or 'best practice' and targeting oneself to emulate it'.3 This definition effectively outlines one of the most important (but often misunderstood) aspects concerning facilities management benchmarking, that is, 'targeting' or taking action in order to release value to the organization. Facilities managers should fully understand the reasons why they are embarking on a benchmarking exercise; they are often forced into following a market trend, an organizational mandate, or the potentially dangerous misbelief that at the end of the exercise costs can be cut. Of course, benchmarking is about saving costs, where possible, but it is also about performance and value, and fundamentally, customer requirements.

The need for benchmarking within organizations can also be linked directly to the competitive environment in which they operate. Globalization and information and communications technology advances inevitably mean that organizations must be increasingly dynamic in order to stave off the competition. Over the past 20 years there has been a business performance revolution which has been characterized by the introduction of methodologies and techniques such as activity-based costing, the balanced scorecard, the business excellence model, the performance pyramid and shareholder value frameworks, all of which are approaches that many facilities managers will have experienced or even feared.

The techniques discussed above are useful when talking about the value chain that exists within organizations where the facilities management department or its activities could be described as a critical link. The techniques ultimately provide strategic management information through the use of performance measures (in various proportions and mixes) associated with the following issues/themes:

- stakeholders' (e.g. investors/shareholders, regulators, suppliers, employees)
- satisfaction/contribution
- leadership (e.g. experience, skill)
- company policies and strategies
- processes, skills, policies and procedures (e.g. time, quality, safety, waste efficiency)
- cost drivers (e.g. resource, productivity, supply chain)
- financial (e.g. cost of capital, share earnings, profitability, operating costs)
- capabilities (e.g. technology absorption)
- innovation and learning (e.g. training and development)
- customer satisfaction, loyalty and profitability.

MISINTERPRETING THE VALUE OF BENCHMARKING

It is common for benchmarking to be incorrectly mixed up with performance measurement techniques. The truth, however, is that benchmarking is a systematic process of evaluation; it should be a fluid methodology that uses performance criteria (among other measurements) in the search for improvement beyond best practice. Within the facilities management discipline this misconception is prevalent, largely as a result of facilities managers often viewing occupancy costs as their only output, rather than taking the wider view of adding value to the organization by providing support through accommodation, workplaces and services. In addition, facilities managers always try to rely on general indicators that are typically available in the public domain. Those who understand the nature of facilities management service provision will readily understand that this comparison provides no value at all, since different cost levels are driven by individual building/location characteristics and the quality of services provision.

The wider perspective Facilities managers need to add value to the organizational value chain. There needs to be a realization that the discipline of facilities management encompasses much more than cost alone. True facilities management benchmarking activities can be largely associated with evaluation of the following aspects:

- assets
- inputs
- processes
- outputs
- systems

Buildings are significant assets to many organizations and the facilities manager would typically be concerned with such issues as physical, functional and financial performance. In this respect there are many methods of evaluating asset performance and feeding information into the benchmarking process. For example, building condition, post-occupancy evaluation, building quality assessment and investment appraisal techniques are all capable of providing data for comparative evaluation. Furthermore, the relatively simple analysis of space utilization is often overlooked, although this in fact influences many of the other issues listed above.

Inputs can be associated with processes and outputs and can relate to many different circumstances within the remit of a facilities manager. For example, the procurement of a new building would be a discrete project with inputs and various activities interacting to make identifiable processes, the final output being the asset or building. The principal inputs in this case would be the labor and materials being used throughout the construction process. The provision of a catering service would normally depend on various inputs such as catering staff labor and raw food ingredients, the outputs being meals, and so on. Possible measures that a facilities manager may wish to use during the course of input/process/output benchmarking could relate to (examples given are as applied to security service provision):

- cost (e.g. hourly cost of guarding, cost of surveillance activities, total cost of security per annum)
- quality (e.g. employee skill/experience level, accuracy of intelligence reports, number of shoplifters apprehended or customer satisfaction)
- time (e.g. surveillance hours per annum, time taken to assimilate intelligence information, time to apprehend thieves)
- risk (e.g. health and safety breach by security staff, injury to third parties due to an unplanned activity, excessive loss to the business through theft)

Systems refer to the mechanisms that are in place to assist with the efficiency of processes. In the case of a new building project an example might be a web-based information system for sharing project knowledge. In relation to facilities management service delivery activities a computer-aided facilities management (CAFM) system should collect information to assist with the management of processes. Measurements relating to time, cost, quality and risk may equally be applicable in the case of systems.

The facilities audit the facilities audit represents a review of the costs of providing office space and services within an organization. It is important to realize that the audit is not concerned with cost alone, but also includes analysis of the building and organizational characteristics that drive cost (resource drivers) and the associated levels of performance.

RESOURCE DRIVERS

A resource driver is a characteristic that influences the required levels and/or deployment of a resource. It is important for the facilities manager to understand that output performance (for example, how clean a building is) may remain at the same level even though the level of resource required (for example, the number of cleaners and frequency of cleaning operations) varies in different buildings (an otherwise comparable building may, for example, be located beside an area of pollution which increases the amount of dirt accumulating on the glazing).

Resource drivers have been classified as:

- quantitative: usually relating to characteristics of the building or organization that can be readily measured, for example, floor area, window area, number of staff and contractors' staff, number of covers served in a restaurant
- qualitative: characteristics such as the location of the building or the specific preferences or aspirations of the organization
- economic, for example, interest rates and market conditions
- operating conditions, for example, specific lease conditions and organizational aspirations.

Performance Data

Performance characteristics are important within benchmarking in order to identify the level of output associated with cost. Unfortunately, many organizations do not record sufficient performance-related information (although this is changing in the advent of developments in CAFM and helpdesk software), and in any case it is difficult to make comparisons between organizations which measure performance metrics differently or not at all. In such cases the facilities manager has the difficult and subjective job of comparing and measuring performance. Customer satisfaction surveys can provide a quick means of procuring performance data.

Cost data

The retrieval of cost data will be a relatively simple process for the facilities manager who has developed and maintained facilities service budgets at a detailed level It is recommended that facilities costs are audited or collected at the greatest level of detail possible. This will ensure that the facilities manager understands what is included within an overall service cost. For example, from an accountancy point of view, a stationery budget may include reprographics supplies, whereas for the purpose of facilities management benchmarking it is often accounted for under the reprographics cost center. It is often a lack of such understanding that leads to the failure of many commercial benchmarking groups or partnerships.

Parameters

Parameters are the metrics that are used to express benchmarked costs in a meaningful way. In order to provide useful statistics, it is necessary to establish a direct relationship between the parameter and the cost of service. For example, it is unlikely that vending costs can be related to floor space, whereas there will, under normal circumstances, be a directly proportional relationship with the number of staff or occupants using the building in a 24-hour period. Similarly, it is common to express the costs associated with premises services on a cost per square meter of floor area, and support services such as catering, mail distribution and stationery are commonly expressed as costs per capita.

Parameters must be measured on a comparable basis between the organization and its peer group. The RICS Code of Measurement Practice provides a standard protocol for floor space measurements that has been readily adopted within the industry. It should be noted that it is common for different countries to have slight deviations from this standard. Comparing facilities costs using incorrect and incompatible parameters renders the benchmarking process ineffective. Services maintenance costs can be seen to vary significantly (in benchmarking terms) because of the use of GIA and NIA; it is a common error for facilities managers to use the wrong parameter by mistake. All too often, professional and managerial reports relating to premises and facilities are littered with incorrectly described floor area measurements. This is also a common reason for commercial benchmarking partnerships failing.

Chapter 2 : MAINTENANCE AND REPAIR

All properties and facilities need maintaining and, for many, maintenance is at the core of the facilities management role. Organizations are beginning to realize that planned preventive maintenance (PM) is more economical than ad hoc replacement of parts when they fail. As well as ensuring that a planned maintenance schedule is effective, managers must be careful to comply with statutory requirements relating to both electrical systems' testing and workers' safety. Facilities managers also need a strategy in place for maintaining critical information technology (IT) equipment. Whereas vendor-specific service agreements offer excellent service and assurance, such provision is compromised when a number of products from different vendors exist within one workplace.

What solutions are available to the facilities manager, concerned with keeping the administrative burden of dealing with contracts to a minimum and ensuring that downtime does not affect the bottom line?

STATUTORY REQUIREMENTS

A growing number of larger companies, local authorities and other public bodies have been pursuing increasingly formalized procedures for checking the health and safety standards of contractors wishing to work for them. This process has been accelerated by the introduction of regulations which require organizations to satisfy themselves that potential principal contractors are capable of dealing with the health and safety issues associated with projects relating to their premises Do note the important issue of statutory maintenance tasks. Failure to check your equipment, system or process and record the results at the prescribed frequencies is serious. There are also certain facilities, such as lifts or elevators, where insurance implications mean that a relevant official has to inspect the system during the maintenance process.

Types of Maintenance

According to British Standards, maintenance is a combination of all technical and associated administrative actions needed to retain an item or system in (or restore it to) a state in which it can perform its required function efficiently and as expected. Essentially, there are two types of maintenance:

- planned (programmed, preventive and cyclical)
- unplanned (reactive, normal response and emergency response).

Planned Maintenance

Planned maintenance is a maintenance organized and executed with forethought, control and application of records. It encompasses condition-based maintenance, which is progressed following information received about a system or structure's condition from routine or continuous monitoring processes. PM concerns the care and servicing by personnel for the purpose of maintaining equipment and facilities in satisfactory operating condition by providing for systematic inspection, detection and correction of incipient failures before they occur or before they develop into major defects. It includes tests, measurements, adjustments and parts replacement, performed specifically to prevent faults from occurring. While PM is generally considered to be worthwhile, it is important to note that there are risks such as equipment failure or human error involved when performing PM, just as in any maintenance operation. PM is also sometimes augmented by reliability-centered maintenance, which attempts to determine the best PM tasks, and by predictive maintenance, which models past behavior to predict failures.

To simplify matters, PM is conducted to keep equipment working and/or extend the life of the equipment, while corrective maintenance, sometimes called 'repair', is conducted to get equipment working again: it concerns actions carried out to restore a defective item to a specified condition, or tests, measurements and adjustments made to remove or correct a fault.

Unplanned Maintenance

Unplanned maintenance includes breakdown, corrective and emergency maintenance. A repair is the restoration of an item or system to an acceptable state through renewing, replacing or mending worn-out or damaged parts. It is typically considered that the ups and downs of unplanned maintenance work should be run alongside planned work schedules. The reaction to unknown and unplanned events can thus be offset against meeting statutory obligations and service needs.

Condition Assessments

Sound property management involves regularly checking a building's health. Condition assessments are now recognized as key tools for both strategic capital planning and tactical project prioritization. Such systems integrate life-cycle data and condition assessment information with other facilities management technology systems, such as computerized monitoring and management systems and project management software.

Facilities managers can identify problems at their earliest stages and evaluate a building's future maintenance and repair needs through a systematic approach to assessing the condition of a variety of building components and systems. These may include building structure, building envelope, mechanical systems, electrical systems, interior finishes and lift safety. Building assessment protocols are applied to each component or system defining the scope of the audit for that category, the procedure to be followed and items that should typically be measured.

Check sheets highlighting potential problem areas should be provided to assist facilities managers in conducting the assessments. From there, facilities managers will be able to judge how much work would be involved in repairing areas that require attention.

Managing The Maintenance Schedule

- Check to see whether any statutory obligations have to be complied with.

- Find out exactly what plant and equipment there is within the estate and produce a detailed asset register (this will probably be computerized), which should be checked and updated regularly.

- Ensure that all health and safety regulations are being followed.

- Conduct a risk assessment on all systems and tasks.

- Make sure that all systems and components essential to the company's business continuity plan are known and that they are properly included in maintenance priorities.

- Develop a planned preventive maintenance schedule for all essential items of equipment, systems and fittings.

- Make sure that an accessible maintenance and test–result recording and documentation system is operational.

- Set up a helpdesk (or at least a work request system) that links to all other procedures and systems within a company.

- Anticipate unplanned maintenance work and agree relevant charging structures.

- Make friends with the finance director, as capital investment budgets will need to be drawn up and life-cycle costing exercises undertaken.

- Keep your team informed.

- Talk to your customers. Ask them what they think of your services (by conducting regular surveys) and find out what they want.

PREVENTIVE MAINTENANCE PROGRAMMED

A Preventive Maintenance (PM) programmed allocates specific maintenance tasks to particular periods in a timetable. PM programmed save money and eliminate downtime. PM programmed range from basic essential checks to comprehensive tests run according to manufacturers' specifications. In general, full maintenance programmed are carried out at the end of a season when systems are shut down after several months of operation. This ensures readiness for the next period of operation. Ideally, a system should also be checked out immediately before start-up to make sure that it is ready when needed. This applies particularly to heating systems in hotels, but is equally valid in industrial premises. Providing site owners authorize a full inspection and maintenance programmed, with replacement of parts where required, they should be able to rely on the findings of such a programmed for the forthcoming season of operation.

READING THE SIGNS

Maintenance engineers should be trained to spot the tell-tale signals from ionization probes and ultraviolet cells which indicate the condition of parts of a system. They should also take full-load current and bearing temperature readings from system motors, which verify their state of health. Companies new to this process are recommended to have a full inventory check or technical audit of the heating, plumbing and ventilating plant at a site. A planned preventive maintenance schedule can then be worked out to cover all the equipment.

This may, for example, require inspection of oil burners every three months. If the planned maintenance schedule complies with the manufacturer's specifications, the system is unlikely to malfunction. However, any deviation from these specifications – any cutting corners or cost savings will inevitably result in unplanned maintenance problems and increased costs. System operating costs will increase with the age of the system, as will maintenance costs and system downtime.

FAULTS WITH NEW INSTALLATIONS

Of course, installing a brand-new system is no guarantee of trouble-free operation and new systems also require planned maintenance. The frequency of major failures due to poor installation or inadequate design is surprisingly high. This is where a site survey procedure often highlights system faults and design defects, which can be rectified economically early in the life of the system. Before the end of the first year of operation, it makes sense to have all the building systems checked for defects, while the property maintenance remains liable for rectifying any installation faults. It is common to find access control panels that are not wired correctly, and missing thermostats.

SPARE PARTS HOLDING

To support the maintenance programmed, a minimum spares holding is recommended. This would include belts for motor drives, inexpensive items but nevertheless essential for the system to operate correctly.

AIR CONDITIONING

PM is equally valid for air conditioning systems. Filter elements need replacing regularly or the consequences can be costly. One company had a unit with a badly blocked filter element, which had been pulled out of its track and was resting on the drive belt. Friction burn marks were evident on the element.

This might have caused a serious fire but was, fortunately, spotted in time. The antidote is to maintain a spare parts holding of filter elements, costing $200. A spare parts holding of under $1000 guarantees minimal maintenance costs, and assures minimal downtime and system reliability, insurance which is well worth considering.

TEST INSTRUMENTATION

Sophisticated monitoring equipment is essential. All engineers should carry flue gas analyzers and be able to interpret the results to achieve safety and maximum efficiency. This can often save money over time. Engineers have been known to encounter boilers that are operating at efficiency levels as low as 40 per cent, when they should be operating at about 80 per cent. This increases the fuel consumption of the system and, more importantly, can lead to blocked and soothed-up flues which, in turn, can lead to carbon monoxide emission hazards.

STAFF TRAINING NEEDS

Frequently, there are basic maintenance procedures which can be carried out by staff without the need for a maintenance engineer. These range from the act of pressing a boiler reset button to restarting an entire system. For example, replacing filter elements at prescribed intervals is a relatively simple task which can realistically be carried out in-house, provided the necessary instruction has been provided. When it comes to complex computer-based building management systems, property managers need to be able to interpret the mass of information they are provided with and training is, again, a key requirement.

Environmental Issues

Some of the latest sites have been designed to reduce certain gaseous emissions, which are known to affect the composition of the ozone layer. Awareness of gaseous emissions is something with which everyone in the industry should be increasingly concerned. There may also be future standards for the operation of energy controls, including those applying to building management systems.

Turnkey Service Management

When buying a new electrical appliance, facilities managers must decide whether to take out a service management agreement. With technology advancing at exponential rates, and appliances now supporting more and more critical applications, any downtime due to appliance failure becomes less and less acceptable. Yet, despite manufacturers' claims, nothing is infallible. There will be occasions (albeit infrequent) when problems arise and repairs are necessary. This is when the service engineer becomes your best friend.

Manufacturers offer numerous after-sales packages to provide users with the assurance that, should a product suffer from a failure of some kind, a service engineer will be on standby to offer assistance. Domestically speaking, such service management agreements (usually defined as extended warranty packages) may initially appear costly, but when weighed against an independent engineer's call-out and hourly charges, they could bring benefits after only a single use. Within the corporate arena, service management agreements play a more integral role in the initial purchase of a product. When committing to purchase a new piece of equipment, assurance is necessary not only that the organization is purchasing at the best price available, but also that the equipment is accompanied by a comprehensive service package. In the event of failure, the cost to the organization in loss of productivity alone could easily outstrip the initial capital outlay for the equipment.

Chapter 3 : PROCUREMENT MANAGEMENT

A centralized procurement system can present challenges for the facility manager. The operational elements (of which the facility manager is one) generally function from one set of priorities, while procurement officers frequently operate from another. Thus, an effective procurement operation depends largely on the successful integration of these two sets of priorities. For the most part, the user is chiefly concerned with the quality of goods and services, response time, and reduced paperwork. Users may not always give primary consideration to price. Depending on the urgency of a request and the tradeoffs among speed, quality of service, and cost, facility department users may sometimes wish to forgo competitive bidding and specify a preferred vendor. The procurement officer, on the other hand, must follow procurement procedures, particularly in the public sector. These procedures include open competition, fair and equal treatment of all bidders, and cost-effectiveness. The procurement officer must be concerned principally with the cost-effectiveness of the procurement function since he is judged primarily on his success in controlling costs.

Fortunately, most procurement departments have become more service-oriented than they were two decades ago. However, a natural tension will always exist. If you understand these different priorities and are willing to negotiate, explore alternatives, and compromise, you'll ensure a procurement system that meets both your and your organization's objectives. Reduced to its basics, the procurement process is a response to the need for goods or services. Goods are normally obtained through agreements called purchase orders (PO), either for a one-time purchase or for a period of time (blanket purchase order, or BPO). During the term of a BPO, orders can be placed against the BPO and are limited only by a cumulative dollar figure.

Services are normally obtained through agreements whose contents vary widely but at a minimum spell out the scope of services to be provided, the term of the agreement, and the basis for compensation. The term may be fixed or may set a certain total dollar value. The price may be stated as a fixed amount or may be an estimate that cannot be exceeded without a formal change to the agreement. All such contractual documents should contain a time frame for performance, a basis for costing, specifications describing the goods or services being acquired, and the general and special conditions. General conditions set the legal framework for the relationship between the company and the vendor. The agreements are prepared by the purchasing department and reviewed by the legal department, as necessary. The terms and conditions of a purchase order are preestablished and incorporated into the PO. For the most part, these conditions do not change. Special conditions are those that relate to a specific procurement and contain specially written paragraphs that define such items as working hours, security requirements, and special access. These provisions are prepared by the purchasing department staff, based on specific requirements the facility manager identifies. For simple contracts, the general and special conditions are often encapsulated in the agreement part of the contract; for complex procurements, the special conditions may be incorporated in the performance work statement.

More contracts today are focused on results and with the growth and sophistication of service providers, it is often better to look for performance-based contracts than prescriptive ones. Prescriptive contracts outline the exact specification expected or detail acceptable ranges. Our experience has been, where possible, to allow some flexibility; too prescriptive a contract leads to lack of innovation and reduced motivation on the part of the vendor. Facility managers need to clearly describe the results expected but leave room for the vendor to create new and better ways of providing service. This often provides for unanticipated Improvements, increased pride from the vendors and staff, as well as potential improvements in the contractual relationship. How much flexibility to allow your contractor is a difficult decision for the facility managers and is best determined through experience.

THE PROCUREMENT PROCESS

Current business literature is full of references to a major realignment of how companies will operate in the near future, i.e., non-core functions will be contracted out with the broadest possible definition of what is a non-core function. Another theory envisions companies composed only of core functions with all support functions gathered under a "headquarters management" function that could itself be outsourced.

There are probably other theories but, regardless, the facility manager:

1) must establish the management of facilities as a core function
2) needs to be a skilled purchaser and manager of outsourced services.

Outsourcing is here to stay and that means that we need to have a well-developed relationship with the purchasing department. Purchasing departments normally are organized according to functional responsibility. It is extremely important that the facility manager become familiar with the procurement officers who handle each type of request. Units having direct impact on procurement are the purchasing and contract sections, although organizations may vary in what they call them. The purchasing section is responsible for acquiring goods or services via standard purchase orders or pre-established terms and conditions. The contracts management section is responsible for acquiring goods and services that, because of their nature, performance period, or other criteria, require specific terms and conditions. FM, consulting services, and multiyear buying arrangements generally fall into this category.

All substantial organizations require a range of support services to be provided which enable the primary business to be conducted. Various sourcing strategies are available to the informed client that demand a considered approach and a conscious policy based on a clear understanding of the factors and features of each.

These options may be considered as:

- **In-house** – where a service is provided by a dedicated resource directly employed by the client organization. Monitoring and control of performance is normally conducted under the terms of conventional employer/employee relationships, although internal service-level agreements may be employed as regulating mechanisms.

- **Outsourcing** – where a service is commissioned from an external supply organization, usually under the terms of a formal contractual arrangement based upon terms and conditions derived from a service level agreement. There may be several of these contractual relationships operating in parallel for a range of services from a variety of suppliers. The responsibility for the monitoring and control of these services normally remains with the client organization.

- **Partnership** – where a partnership or strategic alliance has been formed between client organization and service provider based on a sharing of the responsibility for the delivery and performance of the service, including the sharing of the benefits arising from any efficiency gains and cost savings.

- **Total Facilities Management** – where a whole range of services are packaged together and externalized to a single supply organization which becomes totally responsible for the delivery, monitoring, control, and attainment of performance objectives that relate to operational benefit. This approach demands considerable commitment on behalf of the client organization in entrusting the satisfaction of its support service needs to an exclusive supplier for a prolonged period of time. For its part, the total facilities management company is required to provide a high level of management expertise based upon a clear understanding of the primary business of the client organization.

The final decision on a sourcing strategy, including the mix of approaches that may be selected, will have a direct impact on the overall performance of the organization. This is true, particularly of those operating in a highly competitive market or which are subject to the exposure of a broad range of stakeholder interests. Critical elements of the decision-making process include the appropriate specification of service levels, the vetting and selection of supply partners, the terms of any contractual relationships, and the monitoring of service quality.

PROCUREMENT OF SUPPLIER ORGANIZATIONS

The careful selection of a service supply organization is an exacting task which demands close and careful attention, particularly if the contract is to be offered as a partnership agreement for a broad range of supply services over a long term by a single supply partner. A number of principles need to be observed if the procurement process is to be conducted efficiently and a long-term supply arrangement is to be formed:

Bid process:

- Financial security and reputation of bidders to be investigated;
- All bidders to be considered to be in possession of adequate and comparable expertise and resources;
- Bid requirements to be expressed in a clear manner by reference to quality levels, delivery standards, monitoring and supervision resources;
- Appropriate time to be allowed for bidding to acknowledge the degree of research required;

- Performance requirements to be expressed clearly in terms of a meaningful and comprehensive specification;
- Bidding organizations to be allowed opportunities to offer innovative methods of problem solving or service delivery.

Specification setting:

- Meaningful language which follows industry conventions to be used;
- Attainable standards to be sought which are consistent with organizational needs;
- Clear levels of duties to be established with strict boundaries of responsibilities;
- Interfaces with other supply arrangements to be described;
- Identify any explicit restrictions on service delivery approaches to be observed;
- Clearly apportion responsibilities for meeting statutory obligations, codes and statutes;
- Describe equipment to be used and responsibility for maintenance;
- Identify any special procedures or processes or unique operating conditions;
- Confirm responsibility for training and development.

Commercial terms:

- Describe duration of contract, payment terms, penalties for non-conformance;
- Identify terms of any cost-saving arrangement or benefits arising from innovations;

- Establish procedure for dispute resolution and settlement of claims;
- Define arrangements for variations to contract or any special measures;
- Describe procedures for generating feedback data on cost, performance and quality monitoring.

Quality and performance monitoring terms:

- Establish quality monitoring procedures and reporting mechanisms;
- Describe responsibilities for performance monitoring including any third-party involvement;
- Define procedure for remedying breaches of performance standards;
- Identify back-up or emergency services to be available in the event of service failure.

Where a new contractual arrangement is to take over from an existing one, it is an important consideration for a client organization to ensure an effective transition that does not compromise the continuity of the primary business nor result in an unacceptable drop in standards whilst a new supplier is becoming established.

OUTSOURCING SERVICES MANAGEMENT

Outsourcing today is an increasingly common way of doing business. There are sound financial reasons for not employing permanent staff who must be fully paid regardless of work flows when you can buy in outside expertise which may be able to do the job better, cheaper and more quickly. Facilities managers' time is, therefore, increasingly dominated by managing contracts with external suppliers. This has required facilities managers to develop new skills. Whereas before, facilities professionals had to be multiskilled, multifunctional and good managers of people from a variety of backgrounds, now on top of all that comes the responsibility for continuing to motivate those over whom they have no immediate line management authority, while managing outcomes through a third-party employer with their hands tied by legal contracts.

What is important for readers of this chapter to understand is the relevance of outsourcing as far as facilities management is concerned because, clearly, outsourcing applies to other management sectors of an organization, not least to the core business activity. To achieve this understanding, the reasons for the current popularity of outsourcing in facilities management will be briefly discussed, along with an overview of its scale and scope.

WHAT HAS CAUSED THIS OUTSOURCING FASHION?

For macro-economic reasons beyond the scope of this chapter, organizations began a drastic downsizing transition during the 1990s. Large organizations outsourcing more and more functions to external suppliers. At about the same time the facilities management function was emerging, and with its arrival the outsourcing exercise was extended from core business functions to this 'non-core' business activity. 'Core' and 'noncore' business are used here in a general sense. We will look at this aspect of organizational structure later in more detail. Flexibility to meet changing market conditions became fundamental to business thinking. Facilities management, the management concept of coordinating many previously disparate supportive functions tended to solve one problem, but create another. The internal bundling of services associated with facilities management spawned empire-building. An organization's internal empires are not known for their flexibility, having a tendency to solve problems by recruiting more staff. To maximize the benefits of facilities management it was discovered, by some organizations, that the downside of inflexibility and empire-building could be overcome by the external procurement of services. Furthermore, intensifying competition, together with a global recession, placed increasing pressure on organizations to reduce total operating costs and concentrate on core business functions. Outsourcing apparently offered the solution to these demands, facilitating both efficiency gains and cost-effectiveness. For suppliers, the growth in acceptance of outsourcing strategies by users has come as a major business opportunity.

Successfully working with contractors on a strategic level is another challenge facing the facilities manager. Today's outsourced contractors are 'partners' who 'add value' to a company's operations. Command and control, as a management style, would be as self-defeating here as anywhere else. Partners are looking for long-term relationships, where trust means more than mere on-time delivery. It means sharing cost bases, profit ratios and business objectives. To a degree, it also means sharing information you might prefer to keep in-house. This chapter aims to explain the nuts and bolts of outsourcing, with guidance on the whole process from choosing what to outsource, to writing and managing the contract, to maintaining a dynamic working relationship.

Facilities Management supporting the Organization Core Business

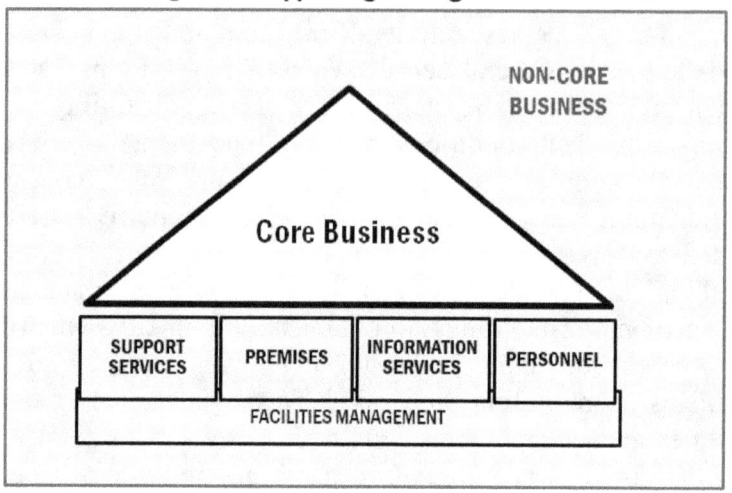

WHAT TO OUTSOURCE?

When outsourcing first entered the management arena in the 1980s, it was all about saving money on essentially manual tasks; premises cleaning was a typical and early example. The focus is now on access to skills, with outsourcing expanding to include areas closer and closer to the center of business; companies are now looking to buy in outside expertise so that they can concentrate on their own core activities, and contract with external suppliers to provide many or most of the tactical elements. The shift from those early manual tasks has seen us move through other administrative and infrastructure areas, towards innovation: how can the company move further ahead faster than the competition? Outsourcing today, and the expertise that comes with the specialist contractors, has now embraced research and development (R&D), design, product management, marketing, communications, even personnel supply and management.

That development has not finished. Already into strategic functions, it is not unlikely that outsourcing of core business areas, and even the strategic direction of the company, could follow.

Outsourcing should not be seen as just a money-saving management device or tactic, but considered in terms of the potential value it can bring to a business. It may cost more to outsource, but the job may be better performed, the company image may be enhanced, and it may release expensive management time for core activities. However, last ten years saw the possible critical turn of opinion regarding outsourcing with some high-profile industrial activities. Some companies are reviewing how they define 'core' activities, which begs the question, 'are we seeing a start of the move to bring stuff back in-house?'. Notwithstanding that development, what, in your specific business, should you consider outsourcing and what should you retain in-house?

CORE AND NON-CORE ACTIVITIES

A first assessment in considering whether or not to outsource is defining what you consider to be your core business activities. Current practice dictates that companies retain control of these areas. The thinking behind this is that organizations should be left to concentrate on their core business activities without the distraction of providing and managing non-core activities. These are better provided by an outsourced commercial organization whose personnel can be better motivated and rewarded in an environment that recognizes their special training and skills.

Of course, what is defined as 'core' will vary significantly from organization to organization. A good example here would be the law firm that outsources its conveyancing work on the basis that its core skill is commercial litigation and it is from the latter that it earns the majority of its income. Consider next the degree to which any selected function is routine and well defined. If it can be easily defined, then it can be more easily measured, and managed at arm's length; and remember, you are not devolving responsibility, just functionality. So, if a non-core function can be defined and measured, it may be worth considering for outsourcing.

People Issues

It is unfortunate that outsourcing is rarely welcomed by a workforce, especially that section responsible for the function being outsourced. Often it is perceived as downsizing by other means, and strenuous efforts are made to oppose it, diverting business time and energy from development to firefighting. Most of the problems that can arise can be pre-empted through intensive discussions and planning. Talk continuously with staff; be certain that they understand what is happening, why, how and when, and understand that simply telling them is not the same as being certain they understand. Do note that when you transfer staff to another company, you send them a very strong message. You are telling them their work is a commodity, which they are welcome to continue performing under new management. You are informing them that your business needs to concentrate on what is really key, and that does not include them or their work. Also, you are telling them you expect to obtain more for less under a new regime.

Business Change

All businesses change. Before entering into an outsourcing contract, you need to consider the following questions so that you are not hampered by a restrictive contract as you pursue your development goals:

- What happens if you are bought out, or buy out another company? They may have a state-of-the-art in-house provision for what you have outsourced, or they may have none, and you need to look at the rapid expansion of the service.

- What happens if you have a fundamental shift in business focus: if you decide, for example, to close a plant, move headquarters of strategically important offices, or pursue a new but promising business direction which affects the need for the outsourced service?

- What happens in cases of force majeure: in the case, for example, of a significant market downturn which leaves expensive equipment and facilities underused?
- What provision has been made to allow for a ratcheting down of the service and the associated costs?

PROCESS CHANGE

The way business is done changes continuously. Think how long you have been using email as a key communication channel. How many standalone fax machines are still used regularly in your business? Do your younger staff even know what a telex machine looks like? Such technological changes can significantly alter the manner in which an outsourcing contract will work over time. For example, if outsourcing had been a significant factor a generation ago, the typing pool would almost certainly have been a prime candidate for it; now typing pools simply do not exist.

It's not just the technology: working and management styles can alter considerably over the duration of a contract. Consider the following:

- What structural changes could affect the outsourcing agreement? Consider, for example, the effect on the catering service of introducing flexible working; or how devolving autonomy from head office to regional offices could impact on supplier strategies, from transport to telephony or utilities.
- What could you be doing for free which used to require specialist input? Think of display media, and how that function has been usurped with presentation software packaged into most laptops, or of the production of newsletters, posters or other promotional material.

COST MANAGEMENT

Whether you are developing a new product or service, designing a facility, providing FM services, managing a data center facility, or changing a key process, it's challenging to forecast and manage project costs or operational costs effectively. FM is a project that is time-bound when you engage a contractor to perform the services.

Facility Management work is considered a "project" because the work is time-bound and the outputs are comprised of several deliverables (identified as key performance indicators that are explicitly defined in a Service Level Agreement). When your company outsourced this FM work to an external provider, you will treat this services contract as a project. In fact, the job is so challenging that half of all large projects or facilities management projects massively blow their budgets, running on average 45 per cent over budget and seven per cent over time, according to consultants McKinsey & Co. For projects in other sectors, the news is no better. The American Academy of Project Management reported that companies were completing only 50 per cent of projects within their original budget. However, strong cost management helps you avoid that fate.

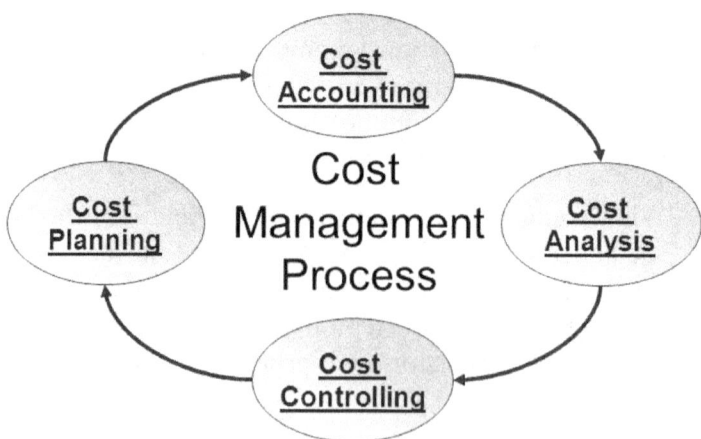

In the context of facilities management, cost management refers to the activities concerning planning and controlling a facility management budget. Effective cost management ensures that the facility management cost is spent within the organizational operational expense budget and according to its agreed scope of work.

Cost management activities are conducted throughout the life cycle of the facility management services contract, from planning and budget allocation to controlling costs during execution and assessing the cost performance upon completion. Although cost management includes a whole ensemble of activities, it is sometimes referred to in terms of more specific functions, such as spend management, cost accounting, and cost transparency. Cost managers sometimes use these terms as loose synonyms for the broad cost management function. Cost Management is comprised of four primary processes: Resource Planning, Cost Estimating, Cost Budgeting, and Cost Control.

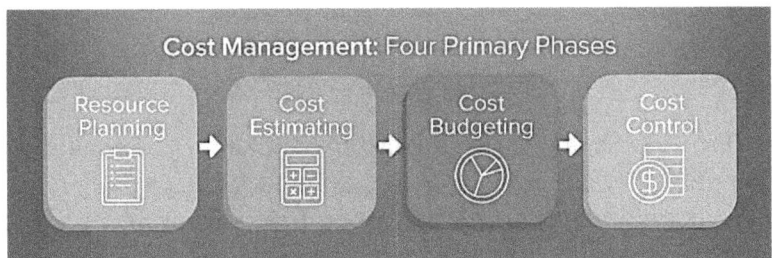

RESOURCE PLANNING

Part of the initiation stage of any facilities management (FM) project, the resource planning process uses a work breakdown structure which is a hierarchical representation of all FM work deliverables and the work required to complete them. This process will determine the full cost of resources needed to complete a project successfully. Managers typically determine the required resources for each work breakdown structure component and then add them to create a total resource cost estimate for all project deliverables.

Cost Estimating

Cost estimating is an iterative process that uses a variety of estimating techniques to determine the total cost of completing a project. Cost estimating techniques vary widely in their approaches to computing project costs, and stretch from conceptual techniques that draw mainly from historical experience and expert judgment to determinative techniques that estimate costs on a component-by-component basis. We will discuss these techniques in detail later, as they vary in their levels of accuracy. Determinative techniques are the most accurate; however, while the estimator's job is always to create the most accurate estimate possible, determinative estimating techniques are only an option if you've reasonably finalized a project's scope and deliverables. As such, you use the less accurate estimating techniques during the earliest stages of project planning and then revise and update estimates as the project continues to be defined.

Cost Budgeting

Once you have created satisfactory estimates, you can finalize and approve the project's budget. Cost managers typically release budgeted amounts in stages according to the level of a project's progress. These allocations include contingencies and reserves.

COST CONTROL

Cost control is the practice of measuring a project's cost performance according to cost and schedule baselines that provide points of comparison throughout the project life cycle. The specific requirements for effective cost control are set out in the project management plan. The individual in charge of cost management investigates the reasons for cost variations if they deem cost variations unacceptable, corrective action will be initiated. Cost control also includes other related responsibilities, such as ensuring that updated project budgets reflect changes to a project's scope.

Cost Management involves Scope Management, Time Management, Quality Management, Risk Management, and Human Resource Management. A cost engineer needs to work closely with a facilities Manager to provide input into the cost associated with delivering the project, changes affecting the scope of the project, risk and contingencies that will impact the project implementation, resources required to deliver the project, the penalty to be incurred should the project timeline is extended, et cetera.

Facility Management Cost Estimating

Cost estimating is the practice of forecasting the cost of completing a project with a defined scope. It is the primary element of project cost management, a knowledge area that involves planning, monitoring, and controlling a project's monetary costs. (Project cost management has been practiced since the 1950s.) The approximate total project cost, called the cost estimate, is used to authorize a project's budget and manage its costs.

Professional estimators use defined techniques to create cost estimates that are used to assess the financial feasibility of projects, to budget for project costs, and to monitor project spending. An accurate cost estimate is critical for deciding whether to take on a project, for determining a project's eventual scope, and for ensuring that projects remain financially feasible and avoid cost overruns.

Cost estimates are typically revised and updated as the project's scope becomes more precise and as project risks are realized, cost estimating is an iterative process. A cost estimate may also be used to prepare a project cost baseline, which is the milestone-based point of comparison for assessing a project's actual cost performance.

Key Components of a Cost Estimate

A cost estimate is a summation of all the costs involved in successfully finishing a project, from inception to completion. These project costs can be categorized in a number of ways and levels of detail, but the simplest classification divides costs into two main categories: direct costs and indirect costs.

Direct costs

Direct costs are broadly classified as those directly associated with a single area (such as a department or a project). In project management, direct costs are expenses billed exclusively to a specific project. They can include project team wages, the costs of resources to produce physical products, fuel for equipment, and money spent to address any project-specific risks.

Indirect costs

Indirect costs on the other hand, cannot be associated with a specific cost center and are instead incurred by a number of projects simultaneously, sometimes in varying amounts. In project management, quality control, security costs, and utilities are usually classified as indirect costs since they are shared across a number of projects and are not directly billable to any one project.

A cost estimate is more than a simple list of costs, however: it also outlines the assumptions underlying each cost. These assumptions (along with estimates of cost accuracy) are compiled into a report called the basis of estimate, which also details cost exclusions and inclusions. The basis of estimate report allows project stakeholders to interpret project costs and to understand how and where actual costs might differ from approximated costs.

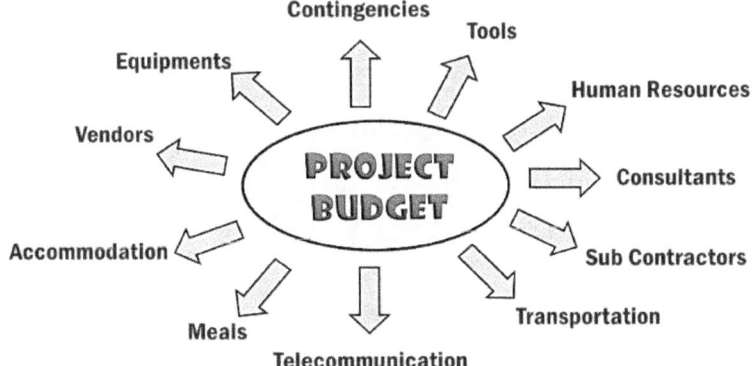

Beyond the broad classifications of direct and indirect costs, project expenses fall into more specific categories. Common types of expenses include:

Labor

the cost of human effort expended towards project objectives

Materials

the cost of resources needed to create products

Equipment

the cost of buying and maintaining equipment used in project work.

Services

the cost of external work that a company seeks for any given project vendors, contractors, etc.

Software

non-physical computer resources

Hardware

Physical computer resources.

Facilities

cost of renting or using specialized equipment, services, or locations.

Contingency costs

Costs added to the project budget to address specific risks.

CREATE PROJECT ESTIMATES AT CRITICAL POINTS

Cost estimates are critical to successful project management, so teams are expected to produce a reasonably accurate and reliable estimate during the conception and definition phase of a project. Estimates are adjusted for accuracy during the planning phase, as project stakeholders and sponsors may ask for revisions before they are willing to authorize a budget. After this early stage, the accuracy of estimates is systematically increased.

Cost estimating is an ongoing process, and estimate revisions are normal in order to ensure accuracy throughout project execution. Typically, work scheduled in the near future will have the most accurate estimates, while work scheduled farther away in time have less accurate estimates. This approach is known as rolling wave planning.

Detailed cost estimates are usually broken down into greater levels of detail and supplementary information. These outputs typically include:

- Activity cost estimates for the activities that make up a project.
- Supporting details, which include assumptions underlying estimates, cost data sources, and cost element sensitivity.
- Requested changes, which a newer, more accurate cost estimate may prompt.
- Updates to the cost management plan, such as those necessitated by changes to the project scope.
- Inputs for subsequent planning processes that use cost estimates.

- **Direct Costs:** Direct costs are those which you can directly associate with a specific cost object. They are billable for specific projects.

- **Indirect Costs:** You cannot associate indirect costs with a specific cost object, and you typically incur indirect costs by a number of projects at the same time. They are not billable to specific projects.

- **Fixed Costs:** Fixed costs are costs you incur during manufacturing that are not associated with the volume of produced output.

- **Variable Costs**: Variable costs are costs you incur during manufacturing that are directly associated with the volume of produced output.

- **Sunk Cost:** A sunk cost is an expense you cannot recoup once it is incurred.

- **Opportunity Cost:** When selecting a course of action, its opportunity cost is the loss of potential benefits from all alternative courses of action.

Cost Management Plan

The cost management plan guides these four processes. Created during the project planning phase, the cost management plan is a document that defines how you manage, control, and communicate a project's costs in order to complete the project on budget. Among other things, a cost management plan identifies the individual or group responsible for cost management, details how you will assess a project's cost performance, and sets rules for how to communicate cost performance to project shareholders. It also establishes the methodologies by which you will control project cost variations.

While you can customize a cost management plan to fit your organization's needs, they usually follow a standard format. Sections often include the cost variance plan, the cost management approach, information on cost estimation, the cost baseline, cost control, and reporting processes, the change control process, the project budget, and approvals. You may also want to include the spending authority levels for key project personnel, specifying which roles can approve costs up to specific thresholds.

Cost Variance Plan

Cost variance is when the actual amount differs from the budgeted amount. In your cost management plan, you'll need a section that details the actions you should take, including who is held responsible in the case of cost variance. The size of the variance usually necessitates different actions: a cost variance of less than five per cent might result in an explanation of that variance, while a 95 per cent or greater variance could force the project to be abandoned.

Cost Management Approach

This section outlines the approach a manager uses for cost management. The level of rigor can vary, but this describes how to establish a cost baseline and how to compare actual costs. You usually track and report costs through control accounts, where you roll up the costs of subtasks. This often occurs at the third level of the work breakdown structure, a tool that breaks a project into small components or chunks of work to determine the resources needed to complete a job or project. However, the point at which you track and report depends on the scope of the project.

Here you will define the methods used for estimating project costs, the levels of variation, and the expected precision, accuracy, and risk.

Cost Baseline

This has a specialized meaning in project management and represents the authorized, time-phased spending plan against which you measure cost performance. It's the sum of the estimated project cost and contingency reserves.

Cost Control and Reporting Process

This section establishes how you measure costs and their key metrics during the project.

Change Control Process

This describes the process for making changes to the cost baseline and how to approve those proposed changes.

PROJECT BUDGET

The budget builds on the cost baseline by totaling the cost of executing the project (including contingencies for possible risks). It also adds in management reserves, which is an amount to cover unanticipated risks or unidentified events that may arise. An organization will usually set a policy for this, and the amount is often five to 15 per cent of the total budget.

Cost Estimation Techniques

Job Costing

Managers use job costing, also called job-order costing, to determine the cost of a product that is unique or dissimilar to other products. In industries such as FM, it's extremely rare for two jobs to be identical. Job-order costing uses a unique job-cost record that compiles total labor and resource costs, as well as applicable overheads, for each task or activity completed as part of a task to determine total expenditures for the job. The job-cost record includes both direct and indirect costs.

Process Costing

You use process costing to determine costs for products or tasks that are identical. Unlike job costing, it does not compute the total cost of a product by summing up the costs of all tasks and activities that go into creating the product. Instead, process costing looks at the processes included in the mass production that creates products. By dividing the total cost of a process by the number of units output, it is possible to determine the cost per unit of each process. After this, you may total the costs per unit of every process involved in the eventual manufacturing of the product. In this way, you compute the cost per unit of each product on a process-by-process basis.

Activity-Based Costing

Activity-based costing (ABC) is an approach to assigning overhead costs to products. Since overhead cost allocation based simply on the number of machine hours needed may be misleading, this costing technique looks at the activities focused on creating a product testing, machine setup, etc. and then assigns portions of their costs to all products created using these activities. Products that were not created via these activities do not have shares of these activities' costs added on.

Direct Costing

Direct costing, also called contribution costing or variable costing, is a technique that only assigns variable manufacturing costs to the cost of a product. You do not add fixed manufacturing costs to the cost of creating a product but instead, associate those costs with the time period during which you incur them.

Life-Cycle Costing

Life-cycle costing is a comparative analysis technique that involves summing the total costs incurred during the life cycles of project options in order to choose the best option. Since starting capital costs may not be an accurate representation of how much a project will eventually cost, life-cycle costing includes all costs associated with ownership including maintenance and disposal costs to enable better decision making.

The first step towards robust cost management is having a clear idea of your project's likely costs. However, it's futile to track and control costs if you base your spending on unrealistic estimates. Project estimating considers several variables, including the method you use to create the estimate, the stage at which you build your estimate, and the types of costs you include. The first variable is the method you employ. You can produce cost estimates using a variety of estimating techniques, depending on the extent to which you define a project and the type of information you have access to. Here are some common estimation techniques:

Estimating - Methods

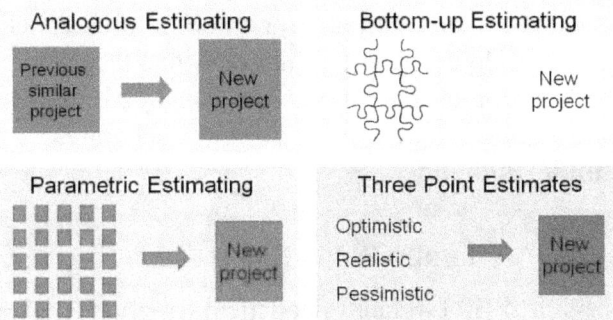

ANALOGOUS ESTIMATING

This uses historical data from similar past projects to create estimates for new projects. This method works if you have experience with projects of the same type.

PARAMETRIC ESTIMATING

This method estimates time and cost by multiplying per unit or per task amounts by the total number expected in the project. The rates are often standard or publicly published rates and can be expressed in hours of work, the amount of data entered, or the number of units of a product manufactured. This technique has a reputation for good reliability, but it's less relevant when the output isn't uniform, such as when writing computer code. Some projects have widely varied or unprecedented tasks, so they do not lend themselves to this method.

Bottom-Up Estimating

This is a determinative estimating technique that estimates costs for work breakdown structure components and adds them together to create a cost estimate for an entire project. The project team members help create the estimate. Since the people who are going to be doing the work are engaged in estimating, professionals consider this method highly accurate, as well as a team commitment builder.

Three-Point Estimating

This is a PERT-related statistical method that uses the optimistic (lowest), pessimistic (highest), and most likely cost estimates to create expected values and standard deviations for project expenditures.

Software-Based Estimating

You can use software-based estimating techniques, such as Monte Carlo simulation, to model the effects of risk events on project costs.

Another factor influencing cost estimating is the stage at which you build your cost estimate. As a project progresses, you discover more variables and actual costs, so project estimates become more refined. You can classify cost estimates based on how well you define the project scope at the time of estimation and on the type of estimation technique you use, the latter generally determines the accuracy of an estimate.

Order of Magnitude Estimates

These are very rough cost estimates based on expert judgment and on adjusting the costs of the current project to reflect the costs of similar, past projects. Created before fully defining projects, they are only used in high-level project screening.

PRELIMINARY ESTIMATES

A preliminary estimate uses somewhat-detailed scope information to form estimates based on unit costs. These estimates are accurate enough to use as the basis for budgeting.

DEFINITIVE ESTIMATES

Created when you've fully defined a project's scope, a definitive estimate uses deterministic estimating techniques, such as bottom-up estimating. Experts agree that definitive estimates are the most accurate and reliable.

The final variable affecting project estimation is the type of cost included. Of course, your project budget must include all the relevant costs for labor and materials, but whether you include a portion of your organization's indirect costs depends on the policies of your organization and the type of project.

Chapter 4 :   OUTSOURCING

Outsourcing facilities management is the practice of giving the management and decision-making authority of a facility to an external company. It can help businesses in a number of ways, including:

Cost efficiency

Outsourcing can reduce costs, especially for smaller organizations, by taking advantage of the provider's economies of scale and specialized expertise.

Access to expertise

Outsourcing can provide access to a pool of skilled professionals that a small organization might not have in-house.

Focus on core competencies

Outsourcing can allow smaller organizations to concentrate on their core business functions.

Risk management

An outsourced facilities management company can identify, manage, and mitigate risks associated with the built environment. However, there are also some potential drawbacks to outsourcing facilities management, including:

Loss of control

Businesses may be reluctant to give up control of their facilities to an external company.

Data security

If proper safeguarding and compliance are not followed, an external company could make a business more vulnerable to data security issues.

Communication issues

Poor communication, a lack of alignment on values, or a lack of relevant experience can cause problems with unmet expectations.

Outsourcing today is an increasingly common way of doing business. There are sound financial reasons for not employing permanent staff – who must be fully paid regardless of work flows when you can buy in outside expertise which may be able to do the job better, cheaper and more quickly. Facilities managers' time is, therefore, increasingly dominated by managing contracts with external suppliers. This has required facilities managers to develop new skills. Whereas before, facilities professionals had to be multiskilled, multifunctional and good managers of people from a variety of backgrounds, now on top of all that comes the responsibility for continuing to motivate those over whom they have no immediate line management authority, while managing outcomes through a third-party employer with their hands tied by legal contracts.

Successfully working with contractors on a strategic level is another challenge facing the facilities manager. Today's outsourced contractors are 'partners' who 'add value' to a company's operations. Command and control, as a management style, would be as self-defeating here as anywhere else. Partners are looking for long-term relationships, where trust means more than mere on-time delivery. It means sharing cost bases, profit ratios and business objectives. To a degree, it also means sharing information you might prefer to keep in-house. This chapter aims to explain the nuts and bolts of outsourcing, with guidance on the whole process from choosing what to outsource, to writing and managing the contract, to maintaining a dynamic working relationship.

WHAT TO OUTSOURCE

When outsourcing first entered the management arena in the 1980s, it was all about saving money on essentially manual tasks; premises cleaning was a typical and early example. The focus is now on access to skills, with outsourcing expanding to include areas closer and closer to the center of business; companies are now looking to buy in outside expertise so that they can concentrate on their own core activities, and contract with external suppliers to provide many or most of the tactical elements.

The shift from those early manual tasks has seen us move through other administrative and infrastructure areas, towards innovation: how can the company move further ahead faster than the competition? Outsourcing today, and the expertise that comes with the specialist contractors, has now embraced research and development (R&D), design, product management, marketing, communications, even personnel supply and management. That development has not finished. Already into strategic functions, it is not unlikely that outsourcing of core business areas, and even the strategic direction of the company, could follow. Outsourcing should not be seen as just a money-saving management device or tactic, but considered in terms of the potential value it can bring to a business. It may cost more to outsource, but the job may be better performed, the company image may be enhanced, and it may release expensive management time for core activities. However, 2005 saw the possible critical turn of opinion regarding outsourcing with some high-profile industrial activities. Some companies are reviewing how they define 'core' activities, which begs the question, 'are we seeing a start of the move to bring stuff back in-house?'. Notwithstanding that development, what, in your specific business, should you consider outsourcing and what should you retain in-house?

CORE AND NON-CORE ACTIVITIES

A first assessment in considering whether or not to outsource is defining what you consider to be your core business activities. Current practice dictates that companies retain control of these areas. The thinking behind this is that organizations should be left to concentrate on their core business activities without the distraction of providing and managing non-core activities. These are better provided by an outsourced commercial organization whose personnel can be better motivated and rewarded in an environment that recognizes their special training and skills. Of course, what is defined as 'core' will vary significantly from organization to organization. A good example here would be the law firm that outsources its conveyancing work on the basis that its core skill is commercial litigation and it is from the latter that it earns the majority of its income. Consider next the degree to which any selected function is routine and well defined. If it can be easily defined, then it can be more easily measured, and managed at arm's length; and remember, you are not devolving responsibility, just functionality. So, if a non-core function can be defined and measured, it may be worth considering for outsourcing.

PEOPLE ISSUES

It is unfortunate that outsourcing is rarely welcomed by a workforce, especially that section responsible for the function being outsourced. Often it is perceived as downsizing by other means, and strenuous efforts are made to oppose it, diverting business time and energy from development to firefighting. Most of the problems that can arise can be pre-empted through intensive discussions and planning. Talk continuously with staff; be certain that they understand what is happening, why, how and when, and understand that simply telling them is not the same as being certain they understand. Do note that when you transfer staff to another company, you send them a very strong message. You are telling them their work is a commodity, which they are welcome to continue performing under new management. You are informing them that your business needs to concentrate on what is really key, and that does not include them or their work. Also, you are telling them you expect to obtain more for less under a new regime.

From that point, the messages they receive will devolve from the vendor's management team, and it is unlikely that these people will be pushing for, say, a healthy information technology (IT) section. In place of the professional environment based on common goals the team once shared, or the partnership with an experienced and knowledgeable organization you were seeking, you will find you have a commodity-based service with goals contradictory to your own. That darker side of outsourcing was experienced at a major global US company which outsourced its IT function.

BUSINESS CHANGE

All businesses change. Before entering into an outsourcing contract, you need to consider the following questions so that you are not hampered by a restrictive contract as you pursue your development goals:

- What happens if you are bought out, or buy out another company? They may have a state-of-the-art in-house provision for what you have outsourced; or they may have none, and you need to look at rapid expansion of the service.

- What happens if you have a fundamental shift in business focus: if you decide, for example, to close plant, move headquarters of strategically important offices, or pursue a new but promising business direction which affects the need for the outsourced service?

- What happens in cases of force majeure: in the case, for example, of a significant market downturn which leaves expensive equipment and facilities underused? What provision has been made to allow for a ratcheting down of the service, and the associated costs?

THE TENDER DOCUMENT

Time spent preparing the tender document is a requirement, not an option. Although you may feel there is only one logical choice for contractor, it is essential that you approach the tender process with an open mind, and ensure that the process is competitive. Do not rule out the possibility of bids from angles you may not have considered, not least the existing function team, and do not assume you know all the potential bidders.

The time spent preparing the tender document is a requirement, not an option. Although you may feel there is only one logical choice for a contractor, it is essential that you approach the tender process with an open mind, and ensure that the process is competitive. Do not rule out the possibility of bids from angles you may not have considered, not least the existing function team, and do not assume you know all the potential bidders.

The process involves three stages:

1) detailed specification of requirements
2) invitation to tender
3) preferred contractor selection process

The first stage, the detailed specification of requirements, is the most time-consuming. It involves a microscopically close examination of the function concerned and a thorough definition of that function. This is necessary because few if any functions of a business can be said to be completely self-contained; all have areas of overlap with other functions, and these must be resolved before you can spell out unequivocally exactly what you are asking a contractor to take on. It may be as simple as defining reporting procedures from company to contractor, or it may involve changing internal processes, between, say, the area being outsourced and the accounts department, to enable an unambiguous command line.

The outcome of this stage should be a lengthy document. It will describe the function in detail, in terms of actions as well as outcomes, and how it dovetails into the organization. If changes are planned or being considered that will affect the function, they should be spelt out here, but not to a degree that compromises company confidentiality. While the document should state that the contents should be treated as commercially confidential, it is essentially a public document over whose circulation you have less than perfect control.

INVITATION TO TENDER

To whom should the document be sent? The second stage, the invitation to tender, can be as broad or as narrow as you choose. One option is to advertise in an appropriate trade journal or newspaper, send out multiple copies of the tender document, and accept bids from all and sundry; more than one company has discovered the perfect outsourcing partner in just this manner, from businesses they would not have heard of otherwise. Alternatively, you may prefer to limit the number of bids at the outset through a preselection process, either through advertisements asking for 'expressions of interest', or through a strict invitation-only process where you involve only a shortlist of contractors already known to you, or discovered through advertising or word of mouth recommendation. The 'expressions of interest' route ultimately come down to a similar selection: all manner of relevant information can be asked of prospective bidders to enable an informed choice of candidates to invite to tender.

FINAL SELECTION

The next challenge is to draw closer to a final selection. You will have received a wealth of information, and almost certainly business references, from several companies, and three or four will stand out as meriting deeper investigation. A systematic comparison is important, as it involves people close to the function to be outsourced; but clearly, this can be sensitive if the in-house team are among the bidders, whether they have made it past the first 'cut' or not. Be sure to establish what each candidate has to offer. You are not just buying another pair of hands, but a functional expert with a brain. If this is to be the partnership you want and expect, it is reasonable to expect them to bring ideas as well as skills with them, and you should listen carefully to their suggestions as to how the function can be tailored more closely to the objectives spelt out in the tender document. After discussions, and sometimes more formal interviews, it is likely that you will be able to reach 'preferred contractor' status with one candidate. This is the goal of the exercise so far and, arguably, where the real work begins.

Final Negotiations

Next in the process is the interval between the selection of a preferred bidder and the contract signing. This is when 'proceed with caution' is a piece of wise advice; this stage can be compared with the period between choosing a new home and exchanging contracts. Both parties have reached an understanding and have a period of time, which their enthusiasm may seek to shorten, to make certain that the decision is the right one; mistakes can be costly.

Sometimes a bidder will fall at this final hurdle. Through a detailed examination of needs and abilities on either side, your goal is to agree on a service level agreement (SLA) which will be your working blueprint for the day-to-day operation of the contract. These final negotiations may reveal incompatibilities, and it is better to discover this before signing contracts than afterwards. Remember that the selection of a contractor is not necessarily a one-off process; you may almost get to the 'altar' and then have to start all over again with a different partner.

Service Level Agreement (SLA)

An SLA is not a summary document, nor is it an outsourcing contract. It is, quite simply, a detailed memorandum specifying the outcomes from many elements of the outsourced function. SLAs need to be defined in detail, as they are an important way of measuring an outsourcing supplier's performance. The most common metrics of quality, speed and accuracy clearly enable each partner to assess the current level of service the buyer is receiving. If performance slides, the SLA may trigger penalties. Putting these metrics in writing provides a legal basis (in the worst case) for contract termination, and gives the client the ability to influence the supplier's performance.

Negotiating an effective SLA that will provide value in the outsourcing relationship need not, and should not, be a one-sided process. The willingness of a preferred bidder to enter into the negotiation of the SLA design speaks volumes for their future acceptance of it, and indeed, they may have as much or more experience in the task as the client. Furthermore, while it is important to specify the desired outcomes in detail, the SLA must not be so prescriptive on the inputs side that it prevents the contractor from seeking ways to do a better job.

An effective SLA:

- identifies certain service levels or performance standards that the outsourcing contractor must meet or exceed
- specifies the consequences for failure to achieve one or more service levels
- includes credits or bonus incentives for performance that exceeds targets
- establishes the level of importance of key service areas by a weighting system.

SLAs are not easy to design or negotiate. But a comprehensive, fair, and effective SLA is critical for a successful outsourcing relationship. In the course of negotiation, outsourcing clients and suppliers have the opportunity to learn much about how their future partner will approach important issues in the outsourcing relationship, which can only help in the smooth running of a contract.

PENALTIES AND INCENTIVES

The most important factor at this stage is for the outsourcing supplier and client to agree on credible measurements, and establish what would be classed as above and below acceptable levels of service. By weighing the impact on key areas of exceeding or falling short of these measurements, to total 100 per cent, then penalties or payouts can be tailored to fit. If the outsourcing supplier, then fails to achieve some of the key service levels, the percentage missed for the month can be applied as a service level credit against a proportion of the invoice.

Often the parties identify a subset of the key service levels as critical. For these elements, the parties will agree that more extreme penalties will apply, even if the outsourcing contract may be terminated if the levels are not reached to the frequency specified. Contract law generally entitles one party to terminate a contract if the other party 'materially breaches' the contract; defining critical service levels and providing specific conditions for termination eliminates ambiguity by determining what is, and what is not, 'material'. Reasonable clients will avoid over-measuring and trying to include every imaginable service level. They should agree to fair credit for failures in meeting service levels.

Suppliers should be willing to understand that the client requires significant protection in the SLA and to acknowledge that there are certain levels of performance that would justify the termination of the contract. Similarly, exceeding the levels may be seen as a potential trigger for bonus payments or other incentives, payable when a quantifiable benefit to the client can be seen, far beyond any expected performance as laid down in the SLA. It is important for the contractor to know that they will be properly rewarded for success. If the supplier can add real value to the client's business, clients should be willing to share the value gained as a result of superior performance. In this way, service-level objectives become highlighted as a critical parameter for both parties.

CONTRACTUAL ARRANGEMENTS

Having established an agreement with a single supplier, the next step is to finalize the contract. Only when all the details are agreed upon it is time to sign. It can take well over a year to reach this stage, and should not be rushed: it is a contract you ideally never want to terminate, so it is important to get it right the first time.

The contract should define both the work itself and the manner in which it is to be undertaken. If the task to be undertaken is ambiguously defined, in terms of both scope (the work to be done) and style (when and to what standard), then there is room for individual interpretation; and one interpretation will almost certainly differ from the next. The contract process is the best system to define unambiguously what is needed and at the same time to lay down performance criteria so the execution of the contract can be monitored.

The SLA is arguably the most important document in the tactical day-to-day management of the relationship. It provides the key performance criteria by which success or failure will be assessed. While in industry practice the SLA is a separate addendum to the outsourcing contract, in law it is not a separate agreement, but merely a set of terms and conditions of the substantive contract itself. In other words, the function of the SLA is to specify the goals of the outsourcing relationship, while the contract is the administrative document which outlines all the practical arrangements necessary to ensure these goals are met.

WHAT SHOULD THE CONTRACT INCLUDE?

As well as terms and conditions, renewal dates and criteria, payment terms, and arrangements for rewards or penalties in the case of overperformance or underperformance (with definitions of these being spelt out), a contract should build in the following considerations.

DISPUTES AND EXIT STRATEGY

Be aware, as indicated above, that there are likely to be disagreements in every relationship has them and there needs to be an agreed methodology for dealing with them, configured in such a way that the work continues while the disagreement is resolved. This methodology should be written into the contract. In the worst possible case, disagreement may lead to a complete breakdown of the relationship, so an exit strategy should also be agreed. In many cases, contracts are expensive and difficult to terminate prematurely. Without careful management, and the right contract in the first place, the outsourcing contractor can easily gain the upper hand, which can be disastrous for the prospects of a long-term relationship. No client should be obliged to continue with an unsatisfactory contract, simply because the implications of breakdown are worse than maintaining the status quo. The client should ensure the existence of a reasonable exit route in case the relationship becomes unmanageable. Terminating a contract is the worst-case scenario in the relationship; ideally, the contract should define less-final consequences for any lack of service or failure to provide to agreed service levels.

CONTRACT MANAGEMENT

Anyone can sign a contract, but unless it is adhered to, monitored and driven to its optimum, it is simply paperwork.

Managing the contract is indisputably the clever bit. It is not the same as managing the same process when handled in-house. Once contracts have been signed and the supplier is providing the service, you have a less direct influence on how the job is undertaken, as you have delegated away the tactical element of execution, except in so far as the contract allows. You can no longer hire and fire, or change emphasis or priority; you have a set of rules laid down that must be adhered to, no less by you than by the contractor. Yet at the same time, you have a team to inspire and motivate, but this team does not report to you. You have to be seen to be interested and involved, to be monitoring and checking; it is important that the supplier shares your enthusiasm for continuous improvement. Unless you are seen to be involved in the contract, without treading on the toes of the supplier, demotivation will follow, leading to declining standards and ultimate contract failure.

KEY PERFORMANCE INDICATORS

If an outsourcing relationship is to be successful, clear measurements are needed to manage achievements and expectations on both sides. One of the best ways to establish this is through the balanced scorecard approach. A balanced scorecard involves goal setting, target setting and an information collection process. It includes a number of categories that represent the most general level of expectations, usually around cost, service and quality. Categories are divided into a number of subsets, known as attributes, defined through a joint buyer–provider process, with the exact composition and number depending on the goals of the relationship and the service in question. Choices are made about an appropriate measure for each attribute.

When establishing the scorecard, some of the key areas to consider are:

- Does the overall scorecard balance long-term and short-term goals, and financial and non-financial goals?

- Do the metrics and measures compensate for each other's blind spots? Consider balancing subjective and objective measures, and qualitative and quantitative measures.

- Are multiple perspectives taken into consideration? Does the scorecard balance the perspectives of the strategic and operation managers, the buyer and the provider, and so on?

WHAT WILL A BALANCED SCORECARD ACHIEVE?

Having balanced scorecards in place during an outsourcing relationship accomplishes at least three things, namely:

- a client-defined, mutually agreed performance management system to reward exemplary service and discourage below-par performance

- an established set of metrics by which performance is measured with the opportunity to make ongoing changes in service levels and expectations

- the provision of historical information to help decide the future of the relationship when it comes to contract renewal.

CLIENT SATISFACTION

Signing an outsourcing arrangement should not mean the abdication of responsibility for business activity to an outside provider. While one of the true benefits of outsourcing is the transfer of responsibility to an outside expert who is well-equipped to handle the task, clients must put systems in place to ensure their own satisfaction with the service. Below are some guidelines for measurement and evaluation.

- Measure what you want to manage: you can only manage what you can measure and you can only measure what you can see. However, it is possible to come up with creative and useful solutions to measuring and managing activities that were previously beyond reach: cost savings and customer satisfaction to name but two.

- Change what you can control: not measuring and, in turn, holding providers accountable for things beyond their control is counter-productive and frustrating for all. The activities and measures must be within the service provider's control and having them at the table defining the scorecard is the best way to understand that.

- Recycle and reuse, do not repeat: the last thing anybody wants is competing measurement systems; a single 'good enough' system will do, defined as providing the information you need to manage with. The balanced scorecard can absorb earlier measurement systems; do not reinvent the wheel, but use the best measures that already exist.

- Set the systems early: construct a balanced scorecard as early as possible, customize it once the provider has been chosen and then jointly set target levels. A provider's ability and willingness to live up to the criteria set in a balanced scorecard can be a consideration in the selection process.

- **Timely and efficient measurement**: the measurement system to support a balanced scorecard should collect only what is useful and not duplicate material. Unnecessary and overlapping measurement processes are wasteful. Collecting information to support balanced scorecards should also happen as soon after the fact as possible.

- **Measure realistically:** be realistic in what can be inexpensively, quickly and easily measured. Certain things should not be measured. For example, do not measure the number of failed state inspections – such events do not provide for ongoing management of the relationship, they represent significant and immediate problems.

Chapter 5: TYPES OF CONTRACTS

Choose the type of contract carefully. The objective is to provide a strong incentive for the FM supplier to make the most advantageous price and value offer to the buyer, considering all the contract variables. The choice of an inappropriate contract type often eliminates bidders or results in prices that are much higher than necessary. The following discussion covers some of the more common types of contracts and explores their advantages and disadvantages. The most common contract types in use today include:

- Firm fixed price (FFP)
- Fixed price incentive (FPI)
- Cost-plus incentive fee (CPIF)
- Cost-plus fixed fee (CPFF)
- Cost-plus award fee (CPAF)
- Fixed-Sum Contract
- Cost plus Fee
- Work by Force Account

FIRM FIXED PRICE CONTRACT (FFP)

A firm fixed-price contract is one that minimizes the risk for the buyer and maximizes the risk for the seller. For this reason, often the seller will attempt to realize a higher percentage of profit in the price quoted when operating under such a contract. This type of contract requires a minimum amount of administration by both the seller and the buyer, and is quite suitable when the task can be well defined and pricing can be established accurately from available cost or prior sales data. A major weakness of the FFP is the incentive it gives the seller to inflate profit as a hedge against risk. In addition, a standard firm fixed price contract gives the buyer little, if any, knowledge about a supplier's cost structure. A provision that requires the supplier to make selected cost data available can be included, but such a clause is seldom used because this objective can be achieved more practically by using several other types of contracts. The net result of this situation is that changes in the scope of a job can easily become extremely costly under an FFP. This situation can be compounded when the contract is subject to several changes in scope after the initial placement. A fixed price contract with economic price adjustment is a common variation of the firm fixed price type contract. It allows for either upward or downward adjustment of the price due to changes in actual costs of labor and/or material, cost indexes of labor and/or material, or published or otherwise established prices of specific items or the contract end item. This type of contract is often employed when the contract period of performance extends beyond a period where prices or labor rates can be accurately estimated. An order that requires deliveries of material over several years may include an economic price adjustment clause. It is imperative that the exact parameters regarding the terms to be used in calculating the price adjustment be included in the contract.

FIXED PRICE INCENTIVE CONTRACT (FPI)

When this type of contract is used, a target cost, a target fee, and a ceiling price must be established. The target cost and the target fee are a cost and fee that both the seller and the buyer agree are achievable. If the seller overruns the target cost, the fee is reduced accordingly. This type of contract requires that the buyer monitor costs closely, though, because up to the point that the seller reaches the ceiling price, escalated costs can increase the fee if it is expressed as a percentage of actual costs (this is not allowed for government contracts). Therefore, this contract may encourage costs to grow as long as they do not reach the ceiling. Close monitoring of all costs by the buyer can curtail this tendency. An FPI contract is suitable when most of the cost responsibility lies with the seller. FPI contracts contain a higher risk element than firm fixed price contracts, though, as do any of the alternative contracting types. An advantage of the FPI is that it allows a buyer greater visibility into a seller's cost and schedule position.

Cost-Plus Incentive Fee Contract (CPIF)

This type of contract, like all cost-type contracts, ensures that the seller will recover all its legitimate costs. In using a CPIF arrangement, the buyer must negotiate a target cost and a target fee with a minimum and maximum fee adjustment formula based on actual cost, schedule, and performance. It is important to agree at the onset which costs are allowable. A CPIF contract is popular for research and engineering development contracts because of the uncertainties associated with such work. Additionally, a CPIF contract allows a shared risk by both the buyer and seller. Finally, its greatest advantage, based on its track record, is that the CPIF is considered to be one of the contract types that affords the highest probability of achieving the desired level of performance.

Cost-Plus Fixed Fee Contract (CPFF)

As in the case of CPIF contracting, a CPFF contract must establish allowable "costs" at the beginning. This is another type of contract for which fee percentages are controlled on subcontracts for government procurements. However, in a CPFF contract, the fee is set at the outset and does not vary as costs increase or decrease. Like the CPIF contract, a CPFF is normally employed in research and development-type efforts that involve a number of significant unknowns. Normally the buyer and the seller agree before the contract is consummated on what the estimated costs of the work are likely to be. The fee is established as a fixed percent of the agreed-upon total cost estimate. This can be a risky type of contract for a buyer to develop and manage when, for various reasons, it is difficult to estimate what a reasonable total cost level should be. Obviously, the seller will be inclined to reduce the risk by tending to overestimate expected costs. It is much wiser to use more controllable types of contracts for follow-on procurements.

COST-PLUS AWARD FEE CONTRACT (CPAF)

Use of a cost-plus award fee contract requires that the buyer negotiate a target cost and minimum and maximum target fee. As is the case for all types of cost contracts, using a CPAF requires that allowable costs be negotiated before the contract is finalized. In this case, the actual fee awarded is based on a relatively subjective assessment by the buyer of the seller's performance, as compared with the specific agreed-upon criteria. In most contracts of this type the fee actually awarded to the supplier must fall within the minimum–maximum range and is not subject to arbitration the buyer's decision is final.

A CPAF contract should provide incentives to the seller to satisfy the buyer's needs. This type of contract, however, requires a great deal of administrative effort by the buyer to monitor both costs and performance. Detailed information in these areas is required for intelligent and fair decisions to be made concerning the fee to be awarded at the conclusion of the agreed upon performance periods. On the one hand, if the amount of the fee is too low, the supplier may find that other existing jobs produce a better profit level, and the job in question may be considered lower-priority. On the other hand, an overly generous fee may create some complacency and attendant performance problems.

FIXED-SUM CONTRACT

A fixed-sum contract requires the contractor to complete a defined package of work in exchange for a sum of money fixed by the contract. Should the actual cost of the work exceed this figure, the contractor absorbs the loss. The owner is obligated to make only such total payment as is stipulated in the contractual agreement. A fixed-sum contract may be either lump sum or unit price. With a lump-sum contract, the contractor agrees to complete a stipulated package of work in exchange for a single lump sum of money. Use of this form of contract is obviously limited to those construction projects where both the nature and quantity of each work type can be accurately and completely determined before the contract sum is set. A unit-price contract requires the contractor to perform certain well-defined items of work in accordance with a schedule of fixed prices for each unit of work put into place. The total sum of money paid to the contractor for each work item is determined by multiplying the contract unit price by the number of units actually done on the job. The contractor is obligated to perform the quantities of work required in the field at the quoted unit prices, whether the final quantities are greater or less than those initially estimated by the architect-engineer. This is subject to any contract provision for redetermination of unit prices when substantial quantity variations occur. Unit-price contracts are especially useful on projects where the nature of the work is well defined but the quantities of work cannot be accurately forecast in advance of construction.

COST-PLUS-FEE CONTRACTS

Cost-plus-fee contracts provide that the owner reimburse the contractor for all construction costs and pay a fee for its services. How the contractor's fee is determined is stipulated in the contract, and a number of different procedures are used in this regard. Commonly used are provisions that the fee shall be a stipulated percentage of the total direct cost of construction or that the fee shall be a fixed sum. Incentive clauses are sometimes included that give the contractor an inducement to complete the job as efficiently and expeditiously as possible through the application of bonus and penalty variations to the contractor's basic fee. A guaranteed maximum cost is frequently included in cost-plus contracts. Under this form, the contractor agrees that it will construct the total project in full accordance with the contract documents and that the cost to the owner will not exceed some total price.

WORK BY FORCE ACCOUNT

The owner may elect to act as its own constructor rather than have the work done by a professional contractor. If the structure is being built for the owner's own use, this method of construction is called the force-account system. In such a situation, the owner may accomplish the work with its own forces and provide the supervision, materials, and equipment itself. Or the owner may choose to subcontract the entire project, assuming the responsibility of coordinating and supervising the work of the subcontractors. Because public projects generally must be contracted out on a competitive-bid basis, force-account work by a public agency usually is limited to maintenance, repair, or cases of emergency.

Force-account work can also be coupled with other contracting methods discussed earlier in this chapter to handle specific aspects of the project that cannot be clearly defined or have undergone significant change. In such cases, the contractor performs the associated work at the direction of the owner and bills for these services on a time and materials basis. Over the years, many studies have revealed that most owners cannot perform field construction work nearly as well or as inexpensively as professional contractors. The reason for these findings is obvious: The contractor is intimately familiar with materials, equipment, construction labor, and methods. It maintains a force of competent supervisors and workers and is equipped to do the job. Only when the owner conducts a steady and appreciable volume of construction and applies the latest field management techniques is it economically feasible for it to carry out its own construction operations.

TURNKEY AND BOT CONTRACTS

Fixed-sum, cost-plus-fee, and work-by-force account contracting methods all require owners to coordinate initial planning, design, construction, and facilities start-up. These tasks distract the owners from their core business responsibilities. For this reason, some owners also contract these responsibilities to the contractor. Turnkey and build-operate-transfer (BOT) contracts provide a vehicle for complete project delivery by the contractor. In a turnkey arrangement, the owner provides the facility design requirements to the contractor, which designs and constructs the facility under a single contract. The single contract eliminates the need for owner coordination and reduces project duration. Upon completion, the key to the project is turned over to the owner and the contract is closed out.

BOT contracts are an extension of the turnkey method. The contractor designs, constructs, operates, and maintains the facility for a predetermined concessionary period. In most cases, the contractor receives no payment from the owner for these services but retains all or a portion of the revenues earned by the project during the concession. This contracting method generally is used for bridges, highways, power plants, and similar projects that generate a long-term revenue stream. At the end of the concession period, ownership transfers from the contractor to the owner.

Material Cost

It is customary for the contractor to solicit and receive specific price quotations for most of the materials required by the job being priced. Exceptions to this generality are stock items such as ply form, nails, and lumber, which the contractor purchases in large quantities and of which a running inventory is maintained. Written quotations for special job materials are desirable so that such important considerations as prices, freight charges, taxes, delivery schedules, and guarantees are explicitly understood. Most material suppliers tender their quotations on printed forms that include stipulations pertaining to terms of payment and other considerations. For the highway bridge project, the contractor will receive during the bidding period written price quotations from material dealers covering specific job materials, such as transit-mix concrete, structural and reinforcing steel, steel pilings, and guardrails. Consequently, if the quantity survey has been prepared with precision, materials usually can be accurately priced. It is not unusual for the owner to provide certain materials to the contractor for use on the project, although this does not occur on the highway bridge. In such a case, contractors need not add this material price into their estimates. However, all other charges associated with the material, such as handling and installation expense, must be included.

Labor Costs

The real challenge in pricing construction work is determining labor and equipment expenditures. These are the categories of construction expense that are inherently variable and the most difficult to estimate accurately. To do an acceptable job of establishing these outlays, the estimator must make a complete and thorough job analysis, maintain a comprehensive library of unit costs and production rates from past projects, and obtain advanced decisions regarding how construction operations will be conducted. Contractors differ widely in how they estimate labor costs. Some choose to include all elements of labor expense in a single hourly rate. Others evaluate direct labor cost separately from indirect cost. Some contractors compute regular and overtime labor costs separately, while others combine scheduled overtime with straight time to arrive at an average hourly rate. Some evaluate labor charges using production rates; others use labor unit costs. There are usually good reasons for a contractor to evaluate its labor expense as it does, and there certainly is no single correct method that must be followed. The procedures described in this chapter are commonly used and are reasonably representative of general practice.

The most reliable source of labor productivity information is obtained from cost accounting reports compiled from completed projects. Labor cost information is also available from a wide variety of published sources. While information of this type can be very useful at times, it must be emphasized that labor productivity differs from one geographical location to another and varies with season and many other job factors. Properly maintained labor records from recent jobs completed in the locale of the project being estimated reflect, to the maximum extent possible, the effect of local and seasonal conditions.

Indirect Labor Costs

Direct labor cost is determined from the workers' basic wage rates, that is, the hourly rates used for payroll purposes. Indirect labor costs are those expenses that are additions to the basic hourly rates and that are paid by the employer. Indirect labor expense involves various forms of payroll taxes, insurance, and a wide variety of employee fringe benefits. Employer contribution to social security, unemployment insurance, workers' compensation insurance, and contractor's public liability and property damage insurance are all based on payrolls. Employers in the construction industry typically provide for various kinds of fringe benefits, such as pension plans, health and welfare funds, employee insurance, paid vacations, and apprenticeship programs. The charge for these benefits customarily is based on direct payroll costs. Premiums for workers' compensation insurance and most fringe benefits differ considerably from one craft to another. Indirect labor costs are substantial in amount, often constituting a 35 to 55 percent addition to direct payroll expenses. Exactly when and how indirect labor costs are added into a project estimate is unimportant so long as it is done. For estimating purposes, total labor outlay can be computed in one operation by using hourly labor rates, which include both direct and indirect costs. However, this procedure may not interrelate well with labor cost accounting methods. For this reason, direct and indirect labor charges often are computed separately when job prices are being estimated. One commonly used scheme is to add a percentage allowance for indirect costs to the total direct labor expense, either for the entire project or for each major work category. Because of the appreciable variation in indirect costs from one classification of labor to another, it may be preferable to compute indirect labor costs at the same time that direct labor expense is obtained for a given work type.

EQUIPMENT COST ESTIMATING

Unfortunately, the term "equipment" does not have a unique connotation in the construction industry. A common usage of the word refers to scaffolding, hoists, power shovels, paving machines, and other such items used by contractors to accomplish the work. However, the term "equipment" also is used with reference to various kinds of mechanical and electrical furnishings that become a part of the finished project, such as boilers, escalators, electric motors, and hospital sterilizers. In this text, "equipment" refers only to the contractor's construction equipage. The term "materials" will be construed to include all items that become a part of the finished structure, including the electrical and mechanical plant. Equipment costs, like those of labor, are difficult to evaluate and price with precision. Equipment accounts for a substantial proportion of the total construction expense of most engineering projects but is less significant for buildings. When the nature of the work requires major items of equipment, such as earth-moving machines, concrete plants, and truck cranes, detailed studies of the associated costs must be made. Expenses associated with minor equipment items, such as power tools, concrete vibrators, and concrete buggies, are not normally subjected to detailed study. A standard expense allowance for each such item required is included, usually based on the duration it will be required on the job. The cost of small tools, wheelbarrows, water hoses, extension cords, and other such items are covered by a lump-sum allowance sometimes obtained as a small percentage of the total labor cost of the project.

To estimate the expense of major equipment items as realistically as possible, early management decisions must be made concerning the equipment sizes and types required and the manner in which the necessary units will be provided to the project. A scheme sometimes used when the duration of the construction period will be about equal to the service life of the equipment is to purchase all new or renovated equipment for the project and sell it at the cessation of construction activities. The difference between the purchase price and the estimated salvage value is entered into the job estimate as a lump-sum equipment expenditure.

Equipment often is rented or leased. Rental can be especially advantageous when the job site is far removed geographically from the contractor's other operations, for satisfying temporary peak demand, or for providing specialized or seldom used equipment. Leasing is a common and widely used means of acquiring construction equipment and may be a desirable alternative to equipment ownership. Leasing can free the contractor's funds, thus improving its working capital position. Under certain circumstances, lease payments compare favorably with ownership expense. Many leases provide that, at the expiration of the lease period, the contractor will have a purchase option if it has continuing need of the machine and if it is worth the additional payment. Lease agreements for construction equipment normally extend for periods of one year or more, whereas renting is usually of shorter term. Charges associated with the rental or lease of equipment items are figured into the job by applying the lease or rental rates to the time periods that the equipment will be needed on the project. Where purchase and sale, rental, or lease is involved, equipment operating expenses must also be computed and included in the project estimate.

Operating costs include charges such as fuel, oil, grease, filters, repairs and parts, tire replacement and repairs, maintenance labor, and supplies. There is some difference of opinion about whether the wages of equipment operators should be included in the equipment operating cost. Some contractors prefer to regard the labor associated with equipment operation as a labor rather than an equipment cost. Others include the labor as a part of equipment operating expense. Logically, it would seem preferable to treat equipment operating labor like any other labor cost rather than include it with equipment operating expense. For purposes of discussion herein, equipment operators' wages are treated as a labor cost and are not included as an equipment expense.

Equipment Expense

As described earlier, direct labor costs are computed from work quantities by combining a labor production rate with the applicable hourly wage scales. Most equipment costs are calculated in much the same fashion except, of course, that equipment production rates and equipment hourly costs must be used. The hourly wage rates of various labor categories are immediately determinable, usually from applicable labor contracts, prescribed prevailing wage rates, or established area practice. This is not true for equipment. Contractors must establish their own equipment hourly rates as well as their equipment production rates. For most items of operating equipment ownership, lease or rental expense is combined with operating costs to form an estimated total charge per operating hour. Power shovels, tractor scrapers, and trenchers are examples of equipment whose expenses are usually expressed in terms of hourly rates. There are some classes of construction equipment where it is more appropriate to express costs in terms of units other than operating hours. The charge for commercial prefabricated concrete forms might be better spread over an estimated number of reusages. Items such as towers and scaffolding are required at the job site on a continuous basis during particular phases of the work, and operating hours have no significance in such cases. Costs in terms time units, such as calendar months, are more appropriate for such equipment items. The charges for some classes of production equipment are frequently expressed in terms of expense per unit of material produced. Portland cement concrete-mixing plants, asphalt paving plants, and aggregate plants are familiar instances of this. Move-in, erection, dismantling, and move-out expenses, also called mobilization and demobilization costs, are entirely independent of equipment operating time and production and are not, therefore, included in equipment hourly rates. These equipment expenses are separately computed for inclusion in the estimate.

BIDS FROM SUBCONTRACTOR

If the prime contractor intends to subcontract portions of the project to specialty contractors, the compilation and analysis of subcontractor bids is an important aspect of making up the final project estimate. Bids from subcontractors sometimes contain qualifications or stipulate that the general contractor is to be responsible for providing the subcontractor with certain job-site services, such as hoisting, electricity and water, storage facilities for materials, and many others. Before estimators can identify the low subcontractor bid (sub bid) for any particular item of work, they must analyze each bid received to determine exactly what each such proposal includes and does not include. The checking of sub bids can be a considerable chore when substantial portions of the project are to be sublet. On the highway bridge, the general contractor has made an advance decision that the painting will be subcontracted. Painting is a specialty area for which the general contractor is ill equipped and has had no past field experience. When such a decision is made, the contractor does not compile the cost of doing the work with its own forces. Rather, the lowest subcontract bid received from a responsible subcontractor will be included with the contractor's other expenses.

The advance decision to subcontract the painting does not necessarily mean that the general contractor will perform all of the other work with its own forces. Other specialty areas of the bridge also may be subcontracted, depending on a number of circumstances. In this regard, the contractor may specifically request sub bids from selected subcontractors, or it may merely await receipt of such bids that subcontractors voluntarily submit. In any event, the contractor must compile its own cost of doing the work involved and normally will be interested only in those sub bids whose amounts are less than its own estimated direct cost. When the general contractor receives a sub bid whose amount is less than its own estimated direct outlay for doing the same work, it cannot accept such a sub bid until consideration is given to several factors. Has the contractor had past experience with that subcontractor, and can it be expected to carry out its work properly? Does the subcontractor have a history of reliability and financial stability? Is the subcontractor experienced and equipped to do the type of work involved? Does the company have a good safety record? The general contractor must remember that it is completely responsible by contract with the owner for all subcontracted work as well as that performed by its own forces.

Chapter 6 :   PROJECT MANAGEMENT

Project management as a function within any organization is a complex and wide-ranging responsibility. The differing activities that require attention through the normal working week vary enormously from the strategic to the operational, and from the mundane to the technical, as at all times, the needs of the core business require to be supported effectively. Given this, the addition of a 'project' into this environment is not to be taken lightly. Projects come in all shapes and sizes, and vary in their complexity, cost and duration. It is important to thoroughly analyses their true depth and scope to ensure that the correct level of expertise is applied. 'Successes for most projects is easily defined by the brief statement, 'on time and in budget'. This disguises much frustration, negotiation, re-evaluation, communication, hard work, etc. that, almost by definition, will be involved. All project activity is normally condensed into a set period of highly polarized activity which dominates daily life and demands constant attention.

If it is allowed to, project management has the unique habit of absorbing efforts to the detriment of everything else, so even greater care must be taken in the approach to project planning to ensure this domination does not affect the smooth running of the rest of the business. The importance of the project to the business will dictate its priority, and how ready the business will be in accepting the disruption it will bring. The staff of the business, referred to in the rest of this chapter as customers, will tolerate more providing communication with them about the project being well structured and they are able to appreciate the benefit in the long run to the business or to their own environment. It is seldom that the luxury of a project in a 'greenfield' environment is possible.

Together with the importance of customers comes business continuity and the overwhelming need for safe access to and egress from the project site to be maintained at all times. To this end a thorough planning exercise must be carried out at a very early stage, to ensure programming takes full account of all known activities for the duration of the works. These activities can take many forms, from known special events to high workload peaks and important dates in the calendar for the department or company. As part of this, activities associated with any other parallel projects must be avoided.

As project success can be measured in many ways, it is best to agree on how customers will determine the success of a project and strive to document what the desired outputs will be. There should be a review to set the objectives of the work and this then needs to be embodied in the project plan. This is to show what critical success factors can be looked for as a result of the efforts. Setting expectations at the outset is important, as it is too easy to lose track of what is to be achieved when business pressures can change requirements constantly. The components of success are important for all concerned this is not to narrow the requirements but to ensure adequate recognition of major change. Good management of this element will ensure the levels of expectation are achieved and recognition duly forthcoming for a job well done. Trying to achieve this after the event is impossible. The main drivers of a project will always be cost and programmed, but a project manager has also to ensure the satisfaction of the customer.

SKILLS IN PROJECT MANAGEMENT

Moving toward a role as a Facility Manager requires skills in project management. A project involves a group of inter-related activities that are planned and then executed in a certain sequence to create a unique product or service within a specific timeframe, to achieve benefits. Projects are often critical components of an organization's business strategy. Projects vary in size and complexity.

For example, they may:

- Involve changes to existing systems, policies, legislation and/or procedures

- Entail organizational change
- Involve a single person or many people
- Involve a single unit of one organization, or may span cross organizational boundaries
- Involve engagement and management of external resources
- Require less than 100 hours or take several years

PROJECTS VERSUS OPERATIONS

In some organizations, everything is a project. In other organizations, projects are rare exercises in change. There's a fine line between projects and operations, and often these entities overlap in function. Consider the following points shared by projects and operations:

- Both involve employees
- Both typically have limited resources: people, money, or both
- Both are hopefully designed, executed, and managed by someone in charge

So, what is a project and how do you know if you are managing one? A project as 'a temporary endeavor was undertaken to create a unique product or service.' Temporary means that the project has an end date. Unique means that the project's end result is different than the results of other functions of the organization. Often projects are confused with general business duties: marketing, sales, manufacturing, and so on. The tell-tale sign of a project is that is has an end date and that it's unique from other activities within the organization.

Some examples of projects include:

- Designing a new product or service

- Converting from one computer application to another
- Building a new warehouse
- Moving from one building to another
- Organizing a political campaign
- Designing and building a new airplane

The output of projects can result in operations. For example, imagine a company creating a new airplane. This new airplane will be a small personal plane that would allow people to fly to different destinations with the same freedom they use in driving their car. The project team will have to design an airplane from scratch that may be similar to a car. This project, to create a personal plane, is temporary, but not necessarily short term. It may take years to go from concept to completion but the project does have an end date. A project of this magnitude may require hundreds of prototypes before a working model are ready for the marketplace. In addition, there are countless regulations, safety issues, and quality control issues that must be pacified before completion.

Once the initial plane is designed, built, and approved, the end result of the project is business operations. As the company creates a new vehicle, it would follow through with their design by manufacturing, marketing, selling, supporting, and improving their product. The initial design of the airplane is the project-the business of manufacturing it, supporting sold units, and marketing the product constitutes the ongoing operations part of business.

Operations are the day-to-day work that goes on in the organization. A manufacturer manufactures things, scientists' complete research and development, and businesses provide goods and services. Operations are the heart of organizations. Projects, on the other hand, are short-term endeavor that fall outside of the normal day-to-day operations an organization offers.

Once the project is completed, the project team moves along to other projects and activities. The people who are actually building the aero planes on the assembly line however have no end date in sight, and will continue to create aero planes as longs as there is a demand for the product.

PROJECT MANAGEMENT BODY OF KNOWLEDGE

Project management is the supervision and control of the work required to complete the project vision. The project team carries out the work needed to complete the project, while the project manager schedules, monitors, and controls the various project tasks. Projects, being the temporary and unique things that they are, require the project manager to be actively involved with the project implementation. They are not self-propelled. Project management is comprised of the following ten knowledge management areas:

- **Integration Management** include includes unification, consolidation, communication, and the integrative actions to control project execution, to manage stakeholder expectations, and to meet project requirements.

- **Scope Management** include the process of creating the project scope document that describe the scope of the project and the scope of the product. The key benefit of this process is that it provides guidance and direction on how scope will be managed throughout the project.

- **Time Management** deals with the ability to plan and finish the project in a timely manner. It involved defining project activities, estimating the resources required to perform the work, estimating the duration of activities, scheduling activities and ensuring adherence to the project schedule.

- **Cost Management** include the processes that establish the policies, procedures, and documentation for planning, managing, expending, and controlling project costs. The key benefit of this process is that it provides guidance and direction on how the project costs will be managed throughout the project.

Project management processes in the absence of appropriate project management knowledge areas will not be sufficient to take a project through the respective phases of the project life cycle. The Project Management Competency comprised of 10 knowledge areas that integrate with 47 project management processes.

- **Quality Management** is to ensure that the project outputs are delivered fit-for-purpose. If outputs are not fit-for-purpose there is a possibility that planned project benefits will not be realized, or realized to a much lesser extent. It can be achieved by developing quality criteria for the outputs themselves and by ensuring that all project management processes are conducted in a quality manner.

- **Human Resource Management** involve planning for managing the people, finances, and physical and information resources required to perform the project activities is vital, no matter what the project size or complexity. For small projects, this planning may not be documented, but for large and/or more complex projects, detailed documentation will enable better management of the resources, as well as transparency for the key stakeholders.

- **Communications Management** includes the processes involved in developing an appropriate approach and plan for project communications based on stakeholder's information needs and requirements, and available organizational assets.

- **Stakeholder Management** involve the identification of people or organizations that have an interest in the project processes, outputs, outcomes or benefits, and planning for how their involvement will be managed on an ongoing basis. It may be done very quickly for a small project, whereas a large and/or more complex project will require a formal stakeholder analysis, a Stakeholder Management Plan as part of the Project Business Plan and ongoing monitoring and review of progress. Stakeholder Management is closely related to communication strategy and planning.

- **Risk Management** describe the processes concerned with identifying, analyzing and responding to project risk. It consists of risk identification, risk analysis, risk evaluation and risk treatment. The processes are iterative throughout the life of the project and should be built into the project management planning and activities. For small projects, a brief scan and ongoing monitoring may be all that is required. For large and/or more complex projects, a formalized system for analyzing, managing and reporting should be established, including the use of a Risk Register.

- **Procurement Management** include the processes associated with contract management and change control processes required to develop and administer contracts or purchase orders issued by authorized project team members; administer any contract issued by an outside organization (the buyer) that is acquiring deliverables from the project.

PROJECT MANAGEMENT LIFE CYCLE AND PROCESSES

One common attribute of all projects is that they eventually end. Think back to one of your favorite projects. The project started with a desire to change something within an organization. The idea to change this 'something' was mulled around, kicked around, and researched until someone with power deemed it a good idea to move forward and implement the project. As the project progressed towards completion there were some very visible phases within the project life. Each phase within the life of the project created a deliverable. For example, consider a project to build a new warehouse. The construction company has some pretty clear phases within this project: research, blueprints, approvals and permits, breaking ground, laying the foundation, and so on. Each phase, big or small, results in some accomplishment that everyone can look to and say, 'Hey! We're making progress!' Eventually the project is completed and the warehouse is put into production. At the beginning of the project, through planning, research, experience, and expert judgment, the project manager and the project team will plot out when each phase should begin, when it should end, and the related deliverable that will come from each phase. Often, the deliverable of each phase is called a milestone. The milestone is a significant point in the schedule that allows the stakeholders to see how far the project has progressed-and how far the project has to go to reach completion.

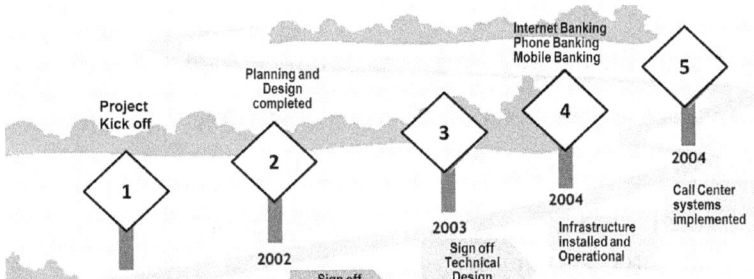

EXAMINING THE PROJECT LIFE CYCLE

By now, you're more than familiar with the concept of a project's life cycle. You also know each project is different and that there are some attributes common across all project life cycles. For example, the concept of breaking the project apart into manageable phases to move towards completion is typical across most projects. As we've discussed, at the completion of a project phase, an inspection or audit is usually completed. This inspection confirms the project is in alignment with the requirements and expectations of the customer. If the results of the audit or briefing are not in alignment, then rework can happen, new expectations may be formulated, or the project may be killed.

WORKING THROUGH THE PROJECT LIFE CYCLE

Project life cycles, comprised of phases, move the project along. Project life cycles allow a project manager to determine several things about the project, such as:

- What work will be completed in each phase of the project?
- What resources, people, equipment, and facilities will be needed within each phase?
- What are the expected deliverables of each phase?
- What is the expected cost to complete a project phase?
- Which phases contain the highest amount of risk?

Armed with the appropriate information for each project phase, the project manager can plan for cost, schedules, resource availability, risk management, and other project management activities to ensure that the project progresses successfully.

CHARACTERISTICS OF A PROJECT

Characteristics of a "Project"

A project is a temporary endeavor undertaken to create a unique Product or Service. Temporary means that every project has a definite beginning and a definite end.

- Have clear requirements
- Have an agreed scope of work
- Have a defined schedule
- Have an approved budget
- Involve resources
- Have some degree of risk
- Produce outcome / benefit
- Create a product or service
- Unique
- Have assumptions and constraints

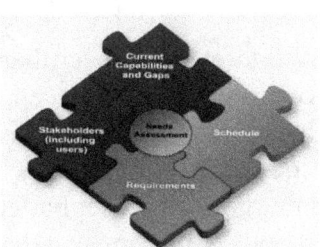

Most projects have similar characteristics, such as the following:

They Are Demanding

The stakeholders, the people with a vested interested in the project, are all going to have different expectations, needs, and requests of the project deliverables. No doubt there will be conflict between the stakeholders.

They Have Clear Requirements

Projects should have a clearly defined set of requirements. These requirements will set the bar for the actual product or service created by the project, the quality of the project, and the timeliness of the project's completion.

They Come with Assumptions

Projects also have assumptions. Assumptions are beliefs held to be true, but that haven't been proven. For example, the project may be operating under the assumption that the project team will have access to do the work at any time during the workday, rather than only in the evenings or weekends.

Constraints are Imposed

Within every project there is a driving force for the project. You've probably experienced some force first-hand. For example, ever had a project that had to be done by an exact date or you'd face fines and fees? This is a schedule constraint. Or a project that could not go over its set budget? This is a financial constraint. Or what about a project that had to hit an exact level of quality regardless of how long the project took? This is scope constraint. All are forces that tend to be in competition with each other.

PROJECT CONSTRAINTS

Project constraints influence practically all areas of the project process. Consider constraints as a ruling requirement over the project. Common constraints you'll encounter are time constraints in the form of deadlines and the availability of resources.

Specifically, there are four major constraints that a project manager will encounter:

SCOPE

The scope of the project constitutes the parameters of what the project will, and will not, include. As the project progresses, the stakeholders may try to change the project scope to include more requirements than what was originally planned for (commonly called scope creep). Of course, if you change the project scope to include more deliverables, the project will likely need more time and/or money to be completed.

SCHEDULE

This is the expected time when the project will be completed. Realistic schedules don't come easily. As you may have experienced, some projects require a definite end date rather than, or in addition to, a definite budget. For example, imagine a manufacturer creating a new product for a tradeshow. The tradeshow is not going to change the start date of the show just because the manufacturer is running late with their production schedule.

COST

Budgets, monies, greenbacks, whatever you want to call it-the cost of completing the project is always high on everyone's list of questions. The project manager must find a method to accurately predict the cost of completing the project within a given timeline, and then control the project to stay within the given budget.

QUALITY

What good is a project if it is finished on time and on budget, but the quality of the deliverable is so poor it is unusable? Some projects have a set level of quality that allows the project team to aim for. Other projects follow the organization's Quality Assurance Program such as ISO 9000. And, unfortunately, some projects have a general, vague idea of what an acceptable level of quality is. Without a specific target for quality, trouble can ensue. The project manager and project team may spend more time and monies to hit an extremely high level of quality when a lower, expected level of quality would suffice for the project.

Constraints are limits or boundaries that is affecting your project activity. Constraints will affect the project scheduling activity.

Category	Example of Constraints
Resources	• Computer resources will be available on a limited basis. • Test environment will not be available on Mondays.
Delivery	• All project documents will require 10 working days for review. • Hardware delivery lead times cannot be confirmed.
Budget	• Local travelling expenses is limited to $500 per month per individual. • Project entertainment expenses is subject to Sponsor's approval

Chapter 7 : PROJECT LIFE CYCLE AND PHASES

The project life cycle (PLC) is a collection of logical stages or phases that maps the life of a project from its beginning to its end in order to define, build, and deliver the product of a project that is the information system. Each phase should provide one or more deliverables.

A **deliverable** is a tangible and verifiable product of work (ex. project plan, design specifications, delivered system, et cetera.). Deliverables at the end of each phase also provide tangible benefits throughout the project and serve to define the work and resources needed for each phase.

Projects should be broken up into phases to make the project more manageable and to reduce risk. Stage gates are the phase-end review of key deliverables that allow the organization to evaluate the project's performance and to take immediate action to correct any errors or problems. Although the deliverables at the end of a stage or phase usually are approved before proceeding to the next stage, fast-tracking or starting the next phase before approval is obtained can sometimes reduce the project's schedule. Overlapping phases can be risky and should only be done when the risk is deemed acceptable.

In a typical project management life cycle, there are five phases:

- Initiation
- Planning
- Executing
- Controlling
- Closing

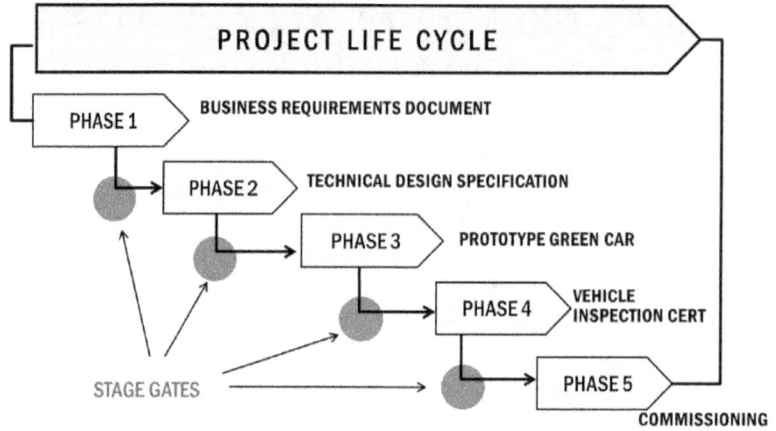

INITIATION PHASE

The phase signals the beginning of the project. It requires an organization to make a commitment in terms of time and resources. For example, the first phase of the project methodology recommends the development of a business case to identify several viable alternatives that can support a particular organization's strategy and goals. In short, the time and effort needed to develop the business case does not come without a cost. One can measure this cost directly in terms of the labor cost and time spent, and indirectly by the time and effort that could have been devoted to some other endeavor.

PLANNING PHASE

Planning is the most crucial part of any project. Since projects are undertaken to create something of value that generally has not been done before, the planning process is of critical importance. The planning process should be in line with the size and complexity of the project, that is, larger, complex projects may require a greater planning effort than smaller, less complex projects. Developing the project charter and project plan requires the most planning activities. In addition, planning is usually an iterative process. A project manager may develop a project plan, but senior management or the client may not approve the scope, budget, or schedule. In addition, planning is still more of an art than a science. Experience and good judgment are just as important as, and perhaps even more important to quality planning than, using the latest project management software tool. It is important that the project manager and project team develop a realistic and useful project plan. Supporting processes include scope planning, activity planning, resource planning, cost estimating, schedule estimating, organizational planning, and procurement planning.

EXECUTING PHASE

Once the project plan has been developed and approved, it is time to execute the activities of the project plan. The product-oriented processes play an important role when completing the project plan activities. For example, the tools and methods for developing and/or implementing a system become critical for achieving the project's end result. Supporting processes include quality assurance, risk management, team development, and an implementation plan. Although executing processes are part of every project phase, the majority of the executing processes will occur during the execution and control phase of the project methodology.

CONTROLLING PHASE

The controlling processes allow for managing and measuring the progress towards the project's measurable organizational value (MOV) and the scope, schedule, budget, and quality objectives. Controls not only tell the project team when deviations from the plan occur, but also measure progress towards the project's goal. Supporting processes include scope control, change control, schedule control, budget control, quality control, and a communications plan. The emphasis on controlling processes will occur during the execution and control phase of the project methodology.

CLOSING PHASE

The closing process focuses on bringing a project to a systematic and orderly completion. The project team must verify that all deliverables have been satisfactorily completed before the project sponsor accepts the project's product. In addition, the final product, the information system must be integrated successfully into the day-to-day operations of the organization. Closure of a project should include contract closure and administrative closure. Contract closure ensures that all of the deliverables and agreed-upon terms of the project have been completed and delivered so that the project can end. It allows resources to be reassigned and settlement or payment of any account, if applicable. Administrative closure, on the other hand, involves documenting and archiving all project documents. It also includes evaluating the project in terms of whether it achieved its outcomes. Lessons learned should be documented and stored in a way that allows them to be made available to other project teams, present and future. Although each phase must include closing processes, the major emphasis on closing processes will occur during the close project phase of the project methodology.

MOVING THROUGH PROJECT PHASES

A project is an uncertain business; the larger the project, the more uncertainty. It's for this reason, among others, that projects are broken down into smaller, more manageable phases. A project phase allows a project manager to see the project as a whole and yet still focus on completing the project one phase at a time.

Projects are temporary endeavors to create a unique product or service. All projects must have an end date. Between the project launch and the coveted end date, a project will pass through multiple phases. Consider a project to create a new electronic gadget. This gadget will have several phases to complete from concept to completion: product description, prototype, revision, testing, and so on. The completion of each phase brings the project closer to completion.

Think of any project you may have worked on: a technology rollout, constructing a building, or integrating a new service into a business. Each of these projects will have logical phases that move the project from concept to completion. The sum of the project phases comprises the project life cycle. A project life cycle is the duration of a project. Consider our project to create a new electronic gadget. Once the gadget is completed, has passed testing and regulations, the project doesn't continue-it's done. The life of the project is over and the goal of the project, to create a unique product in this case, has been met. There's no reason for the project to keep going-so its life cycle is over.

PROJECT PHASE DELIVERABLES

Every phase has deliverables. It's one of the main points of having phases. For example, your manager gives you a project that will require four years to complete and has a hefty budget of $122 million. Do you think management is going to say, 'Have fun-see you in four years?'

Of course, in most organizations, that's not going to happen. Management wants to see proof of progress, evidence of work completed, and good news about how well the project is moving. Phases are an ideal method of keeping management informed of the project's progression. The following illustration depicts a project moving from conception to completion. At the end of each phase there is some deliverable that the project manager can show to management and customers.

They'll want a schedule of when we'll be spending their money and what they'll be getting in return. And when will this fun happen? At the end of a project phase. The project manager will be accountable for several things at the end of a project phase:

- The performance of the project to date
- The performance of the project team to date
- Proof of deliverables in the project phase
- Verification of deliverables in alignment with the project scope

STAGE GATES

Project phases are also known as stage gates. Stage gates are used often in manufacturing and product development. A stage gate allows a project to continue after the performance and deliverable review against a set of predefined metrics. If the deliverables of the phase, or stage, met the predefined metrics, the project is allowed to continue. Should the deliverable not meet the metrics, the project may not be allowed to pass through the gate to move forward. In these unfortunate cases, the project may be terminated or sent through revisions to meet the predetermined metrics. The following illustration shows the advancement of the project through phases.

The completion of a phase may also be known as a phase exit. A phase exit requires the project deliverable to meet some predetermined exit criteria. Exit criteria are typically inspection-specific and are scheduled events in the project schedule. Exit criteria can include many different activities, such as:

- Sign-offs from the customer
- Regulatory inspections and audits
- Quality metrics
- Performance metrics
- Security audits

Project life cycles, comprised of phases, move the project along. Project life cycles allow a project manager to determine several things about the project, such as:

- What work will be completed in each phase of the project?
- What resources, people, equipment, and facilities will be needed within each phase?
- What are the expected deliverables of each phase?
- What is the expected cost to complete a project phase?
- Which phases contain the highest amount of risk?

Armed with the appropriate information for each project phase, the project manager can plan for cost, schedules, resource availability, risk management, and other project management activities to ensure that the project progresses successfully.

COMMUNICATION

The need for good effective communication throughout a project is important to the success of the work. It is essential if the project drivers are to work. It is necessary to determine firstly who needs to know, who would be best to know, and who will assist in the delivery of the work by being kept informed. Finally, there is the need for everyone's general interest to be satisfied through regular briefings specifically designed to inform. The communication plan should form an early part of any planning exercise and it should be tested at regular intervals. Good, timely communication can smooth out inconveniences as they tend not to be readily accepted unless understood and the benefits explained. Being seen to be approachable through regular communication can stop time being wasted. Handled effectively, this will not be seen as a weakness but can mean customers will feel involved. Early information can also help prevent mistakes as a wider audience has knowledge of the activity. It may also ultimately avoid downtime or costly rework.

Projects usually stem from an overwhelming need for some form of change required by the business, group, department or organization. Needs may come from product change, legislation change, staff need, relocation or a host of other reasons. Seldom is this a frivolous requirement, therefore value for money will always be the watchword. Work on a project has always to be affordable and therefore communication assumes even greater importance. There will always be an owner or client who will have the authority to commit the funding necessary for the work, or the changes that may be necessary during the course of it. The speed and effectiveness of this line of control will also drastically affect the overall price of the finished product. Having established the requirements and set the customer expectation level then the real task of evaluating the out-turn cost against the requirement can begin. Inevitably this will require some adjustments to be made to create a fit. Adjustments should be kept to a minimum in any project but the whole plan should take into account what other funds are available for related or adjacent works that can be included in the requirement to get that extra positive contribution. This includes reviewing whatever asset management funds and plans, major repair reserves or any other planner's funds there are to see what might be available to help get a much more effective job. Good communications can help secure finance director support and a good facilities/project manager can bring fresh ideas to bear to give extra added value. All this is required at this point prior to tendering for the works.

FACILITIES MANAGEMENT WORK BREAKDOWN STRUCTURE

A Work Breakdown Structure (WBS) is a graphical representation of the hierarchy of project deliverables and their associated tasks. As opposed to a Project Schedule that is calendar based, a WBS is deliverable-based, and written in business terms.

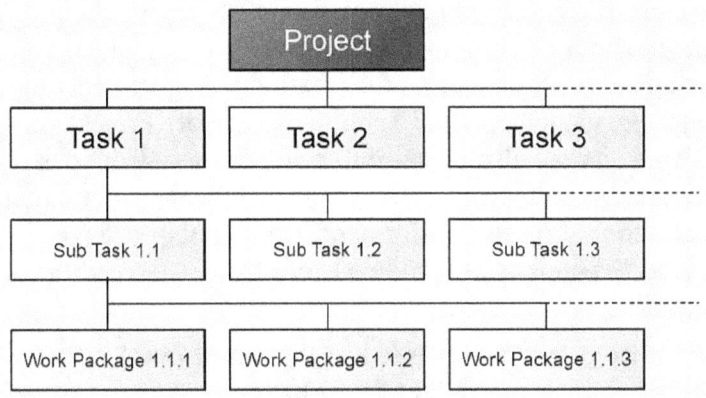

There are no dates or effort estimates in a WBS. Using a WBS, Project Team members are better equipped to estimate the level of effort required to complete tasks, and are able to quickly understand how their work fits into the overall project structure. The input and guidance of the project team is required as they are the individuals closest to the work and will be completing the actual activities within the project phases. The WBS will offer major input into planning, estimating, and scheduling processes throughout the project.

The first hierarchical level of a WBS usually contains the phases that are specific to the lifecycle of the project being performed. For example, the first level and second level of the WBS for a software development project would most likely contain System Requirements, System Design respectively. For this reason, a WBS may be reused for other projects with the same lifecycle. Once the first level has been completed, it is broken down into more detailed sub-levels, until eventually all tasks are explicitly defined. When defined to the appropriate level of detail, a WBS is very useful as input to both creating and refining a Project Schedule, particularly in estimating the required resources, level of effort, and cost. Additional constraints, such as completion dates for project deliverables mandated by the Project Sponsor, Customer, or other external factors, will most often be known early in the project management life cycle and should be noted.

Using the information from the WBS as input, the Project Manager should begin to document effort estimates, roles and dependencies, in preparation for creating a Project Schedule using a project management tool such as Microsoft Project or Oracle Primavera. It may also be helpful to solicit input from past Project Managers, Project Team members and subject matter experts for insight into past project performance, and to help uncover required activities, dependencies, and levels of effort.

BREAKING DOWN THE FACILITIES MANAGEMENT DELIVERABLES

Breaking down the major project deliverables into smaller, manageable components is important so that resources can be assigned, measured, executed and controlled. Determine if adequate cost and time estimates can be applied to the lowest level of the decomposed work. Deliverables that cannot be realized until later portions of the project may be difficult to decompose since there are many variables between now and when the deliverable is created. The smallest component of the WBS is referred to as the "**work package**".

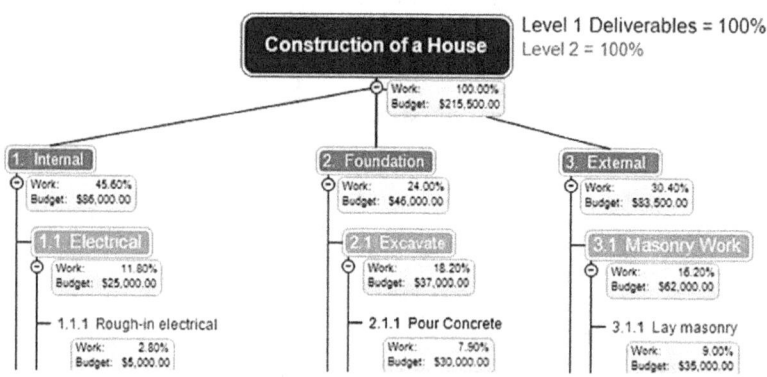

The lower-level items must be evaluated to ensure they are complete and accurate. Each item within the decomposition must be clearly defined and deliverable-orientated. Finally, each item should be decomposed to the point that it can be scheduled, budgeted, and assigned to a resource.

FACILITIES MANAGEMENT INTEGRATION WITH COST ESTIMATING

The job of estimating FM project costs and ongoing budget control is not done in a vacuum. Several other project management specialties influence it, and the cost estimation, in turn, has an impact on those other project aspects. Some of these are:

HUMAN RESOURCE MANAGEMENT

Inadequately trained or unprepared project staff can be a liability in terms of both time and money.

PROCUREMENT MANAGEMENT

Ineffective procurement management can increase project costs, especially for projects performed over extended lengths of time. For example, fluctuating resource prices and changing economic and political conditions may make it more expensive to procure necessary goods or services.

QUALITY MANAGEMENT

Establish quality requirements for project deliverables before execution begins, and communicate these requirements to all project team members. A lack of clarity on quality requirements can prove costly during the quality control process when defects or noncompliance must be addressed (often at substantial cost).

Time Management

Project costs are directly related to the time taken to complete a project, and so a failure to construct an accurate and viable project schedule will likely cause cost overruns.

Scope Management

A project scope is a description of the work required to deliver the product of a project. The project scope defines what work will, and will not, be included in the project work. A project scope guides the project manager on decisions to add, change, or remove the work of the project. The project scope defines all of the required work, and only the required work, to complete the project. Scope management is the process of ensuring that the project work is within the scope and protecting the project from scope creep. Scope creep refers to increasing feature or additional functionality that is not included in the original Project Scope but the additional functionality is very important to the Customer, adding small yet time and resource-consuming features to the system once the scope of the project has been approved. The Project Scope Statement is the baseline for all future project decisions, as it justifies the business need of the project. Control Scope is a process that concerned with ensuring that any changes to the project scope will be managed through the change control process and to verify that the output from the project meets the requirements defined in the Project Scope Statement. A scope change procedure will be in place before the actual work on the project commences. It can be part of or at least referenced in, the project charter so that it is communicated to all project stakeholders. This procedure should allow for the identification and handling of all requested changes to the project's scope. Scope change requests can be made, and each request's impact on the project can be assessed. Then, a decision on whether to accept or reject the scope change can be made. If the scope change request is accepted, a mitigation plan or a contingency plan needs to be defined should the scope changes impact the project budget and the project schedule.

Risk Management

All projects face risks. Adequate risk identification and preparation of contingency plans and reserves are vital to prevent risks from causing cost overruns.

Risk, if not managed, will become issues, however, not all issues are derived from the Risk Register. For example, when a particular project work package is lacking the required resources, it is classified as a project issue that needs to be addressed immediately. It is not identified as a risk because it is mandatory to ensure adequate resources are assigned to all project activities. It is classified as a risk in a situation where the resources are complete but they may lack the skills necessary to perform the job. The probability of the project not meeting its expected schedule is definitely going to happen if this work package is delayed. Management of project issues focuses on monitoring, reviewing and addressing issues or concerns as they arise throughout the life of a project. Issues can be raised by anyone involved with the project, including the business owners, steering committee members, reference or working group members, the project manager, project team members and other key stakeholders. For small projects, a brief scan and ongoing monitoring may be all that is required. In large and/or more complex projects, it is advisable to maintain a Project Issues Register. From this register, the issue, current status, and resolution, where appropriate, should be reported regularly to the steering committee as part of the project status report. A

Issues Management

Project Issues Register should be established as part of the ongoing risk management activities. The project manager and team need to have a process for capturing issues as they arise, updating and reviewing them so that they can be managed and resolved as the project moves forward. Once a resolution is agreed on, the appropriate activities are added to the project work plan to ensure the issue is resolved, and to the project budget if appropriate. If the project is medium to large or quite complex, a separate Project Issues Register might be established for each of the major outputs as they are being developed. Small projects also will benefit from the establishment of a Project Issues Register, as it is low maintenance and high value in terms of keeping the project on track and managing the issues. The process "Identify Project Issues" will ensure that project issues are Chartered in Project Issues Register for closer tracking and control. In the example introduced earlier in this section, the issue raised for not having sufficient resources may be posted into the project Risk Register and to be classified as a risk for not having the required skilled resources.

COMMUNICATIONS MANAGEMENT

Routinely update project team members and stakeholders with project activities. Project team members who do not understand their roles cost the project time and money. Likewise, stakeholders who do not receive regular project progress updates may request costly management changes at non-optimal times.

Since stakeholders can have a significant impact on decisions made, it is important that their perceptions of risk be identified and documented, with the underlying reasons for the perceptions understood and documented. Communication and consultation with all key stakeholders should be an ongoing process and not just part of the initial risk identification and analysis process. This process can be tied in with the overall communication strategy for the project and need not be a separate activity. Information technology projects historically have demonstrated a poor track record for a variety of reasons. Often unrealistic Risk Management plans are created from inaccurate estimates, and, as a result, projects have little chance of achieving their objectives. Although various tools and techniques for estimating IT projects exist but consistently developing accurate and realistic estimates remain a challenge. Much of an organization's capability to consistently and accurately estimate IT projects lies with well-defined processes, experience, and an information base of past projects. Still, developing a realistic and effective Risk Management plan is only part of the solution. Formalized regular reporting on the status of the project is an integral part of the quality management of the project. In order to make appropriate decisions, the steering committee, project sponsor or senior manager needs to be informed properly about the risk status of the project. The project manager should establish this reporting as part of the management activities for the project. In this workshop, you will learn about developing effective communications plan to better track, monitor, and report the project's progress. Communications management is important in ensuring project team, project sponsor, and all project stakeholders are involved in the risk management processes and the decisions made related to the contingencies and mitigation plan. After completion of this workshop, you should understand and be able to identify the processes associated with project communications management, which includes project communications planning, information distribution, and risk reporting.

Chapter 8 : The FM Project Cost Management

Facilities management work starts after the project has been delivered to the client should the client decides to outsource the operational work to a third party. If you look at a FM project, for example, the maintenance of the service elevators will need to be contracted to a third party or external service provider. This is a non-core business and as such it makes business sense to outsource this work to an external contractor.

FACILITY MANAGEMENT PROJECTS

FM project cost managers, or quantity surveyors, oversee cost estimation and cost control while maintaining a project's profitability. They are responsible for ensuring that a project remains within budget while meeting its scope, quality, and performance requirements. Though the majority of FM projects are not subject to the "first-time, first-use penalty," they are still highly complex. And as hard projects, their design, scope, and budgetary requirements must be planned before work begins. Experience and formal training are essential for quantity surveyors. The evaluation and recommendation of bids is one of the quantity surveyor's primary responsibilities, though they may be engaged in a project from inception to conclusion. In fact, quantity surveyors get their name from the bill of quantities, a cost estimate prepared by the surveyor and by which contractors' tenders are assessed.

To aid cost management for large, complex projects, quantity surveyors or project managers may use cost codes discussed earlier to set up multiple cost accounts. These accounts are essentially a portion of the budget marked for specific expenses such as labor, FM materials, architectural design, etc.

FM costs span two major cost categories: those incurred in the actual FM and development of a facility and those incurred in the operations and maintenance of the facility throughout its life cycle. The first category includes things like the cost of land, labor, equipment, and materials needed to build a facility, the cost of architectural design and engineering, and the cost of facility inspection. The second category includes maintenance and repair costs, land rent and utilities costs, and the cost of operations and employing operations staff. FM Project Manager works closely with Facility Manager to derive the operational cost of the facility at the end of the FM project.

One factor that looms large in cost estimation for FM projects is the need for contingencies. Since FM projects are typically large-scale and performed over extended periods of time, adequate contingency planning is vital.

CONTINGENCIES IN FM PROJECTS

- Schedule adjustments, which are not unusual for such large-scale projects. Given the large costs of equipment and labor in FM projects, delays and schedule extensions can increase costs considerably.

- Changes in equipment and labor costs, which are also not uncommon in lengthy projects.

- Environmental changes, such as changes in climate again not uncommon in lengthy projects.

- Changes in design development, which, though rare, are not unheard of. These depend on the quality of pre-execution project planning and uncontrollable circumstances such as natural events.

COST ESTIMATES FOR FM PROJECTS

Cost estimates for FM projects fall into three classes:

- Design estimates: Created during project planning and design, these include a number of estimates ranging in accuracy from screening through conceptual to definitive.

- Bid estimates: This is a finalized definitive estimate used to conduct competitive bidding.

- Control estimates: Use these to measure cost performance during project execution; they are susceptible to revisions during a project.

An important aspect of cost estimation in FM projects is determining the relationship between project scale and average cost per unit. Typically, estimators using empirical data to establish these relationships will find that there are economies or diseconomies of scale. That is the average cost per unit changes as the scale of the project increases. Estimators seek to take advantages of economies of scale to minimize unit costs.

Civil engineering projects (such as for highways and bridges) sometimes have added pressure from increased public interest in their progress and especially their cost performance. This can be problematic when critics fail to appreciate the iterative nature of cost estimating and draw misleading comparisons between inaccurate preliminary estimates and control estimates. This problem is compounded by the fact that civil engineering projects typically feature large degrees of uncertainty in estimates usually due to a combination of project length, natural conditions, and, in some instances, political conditions in the region. As such, organizations such as The Institution of Engineers of Ireland suggest that preliminary estimates for civil engineering projects not be made public and that more definitive estimates clearly state project scopes and underlying assumptions.

Civil engineering projects that run over extended periods of time may also have to contend with scope changes requested by changing political administrations. In some developing countries, these projects might struggle to retain political support as governments change, and it is not uncommon for there to be problems with administrative corruption. As such, civil engineering projects place special importance on adequate risk identification, and contingency reserves for these projects tend to be generous. It is also important to undertake project planning in a way that minimizes the likelihood of future scope changes since these can easily cause cost overruns.

COST ESTIMATES USING PRISM

PRISM is a project budgeting and risk modelling tool that is commonly used by FM managers to derive the cost of managing a Data Center facility. PRISM can be applied to other projects. There are two costs involved:

1) cost of building the data center
2) cost of facilities management that include maintenance and ongoing operations of the data center.

Project cost management is traditionally a weak area of IT projects. IT project managers must acknowledge the importance of cost management and take responsibility for understanding basic cost concepts, cost estimating, budgeting, and cost control. PRISM can be applied in other projects like FM and engineering projects, this tool can easily be customized to suit the needs of Facility Manager, Quantity Surveyor, Project Planner, and others in similar roles. You need to be familiar with Microsoft Excel in order to customize this tool. The standard PRISM has the functionality to capture costs associated with any types of projects.

Facility Managers must understand several basic principles of cost management to be effective in managing project costs. It is difficult to manage risks in a project if you do not know the cost implications of the project objectives. For example, if you are expecting the scope of the project to change during the planning phase as advised by your customer, you will probably allocate some buffer in the project schedule in anticipation of this change, so the project schedule will not be affected by this change. This could be one of the risk response strategies but what about the additional cost related to labor, material, expenses, and others as a result of the changes in project scope? How will you provide an accurate estimation of this cost and how will you make provision for this additional cost in the overall project budget? What is the mitigation plans to control scope creep and what will be the contingency plans should the changes need to be accepted and the functionalities included in the finished product? If you are not familiar with risk management and cost management process then you will most likely be unable to control the project capital expenditure. In this example, not knowing the cost as a consequence of scope changes will result in a high probability of this project failing to complete according to the agreed budget.

PRISM is a specially designed risk-modelling tool for project cost managers to prepare a balanced project budget through the modelling of project budget, contingency reserve, project liabilities, and provision for risks. After defining all costs into PRISM, the risk affecting the project activities, the project selling price, and let PRISM generate the profitability report and risk analysis automatically. With PRISM, you can model your project costing and risk appetite to suit your margin requirements. A complete overview of the PRISM framework will be discussed in this book to facilitate the development of the respective functionalities. In addition to the sleek dashboard that displays a brief and concise overview of the entire breakdown of project prime cost, the breakdown of project cost including risk, and project profitability, PRISM is a user-friendly tool for ad-hoc reporting of project performance. There are several processes to capture all costs into PRISM.

COST OF LABOR

Using "Define Labor Services" process, the cost of labor or manpower services can be easily captured into PRISM. This is the first part of several series of workshops that will be focusing on developing the project risk management tool called "PRISM", this tool will be used throughout the risk management process. The Facility Manager may use manual or automated tools to generate a preliminary project budget.

The Facility Manager calculates the preliminary budget that will be required to complete project activities. All aspects of the project, including the cost of human resources, equipment, travel, materials, and supplies, should be incorporated in the subsequent workshops. Labor cost will be defined based on the project activities in the work breakdown structure. The Facility Manager must also have a general understanding of the cost of both the human resources and the equipment and materials required to perform the work. The method by which human resources will be acquired for the project will directly affect the risk budgeting process.

		LABOUR				
Contractor	GAFM CONSULTING			PRISM Ref.	P1-21-011	
Project Name	INTEGRATED BANKING SYSTEMS			Version	V1.0	
Subject	PROJECT RISK & PROFITABILITY			Currency	USD	
Customer	ABC Banking Corporation					
No.	WORK PACKAGE	RESOURCE	RATE $/day	Effort (mandays)	Amount $	
1	Project Management	Project Manager	3,500	120.0	420,000.00	
2	Develop Design Specification	Solution Architect	900	30.0	27,000.00	
3	Technical Design Review					
4		Project Manager	3,500	3.0	10,500.00	
5		Solution Architect	2,000	2.0	4,000.00	
6		Quality Engineer	1,800	2.0	3,600.00	
7		PMO Manager	1,900	2.0	3,800.00	
8	Data conversion		500	20.0	10,000.00	
9	Data Cleanse		1,000	20.0	20,000.00	
10	Business Object Modelling		600	12.0	7,200.00	
11	Application Customization		500	90.0	45,000.00	
12	Reports Development		600	30.0	18,000.00	
13	Unit testing		300	20.0	6,000.00	
14	System Integration Testing		700	25.0	17,500.00	
15	User Acceptance Testing		800	20.0	16,000.00	
16	Training		990	8.0	7,920.00	
17	Preparation for rollout		450	30.0	13,500.00	
18	Development and Test Environment setup		950	15.0	14,250.00	
19	Documentation		400	30.0	12,000.00	
20	Support during warranty period		500	60.0	30,000.00	
21						
22						
23						
	Total Effort (in man-days)	539.0		LABOUR	686,270.00	

PRISM will assist the project cost manager and project team to manage project risk from the System Requirements phase until System Transition phase of the system development life cycle. As for other projects that is not associated with software development, PRISM will manage the risk according to the phases in the project management life cycle i.e., from Project Initiation phase until Project Closure.

Although the cost of labor will be captured for all work packages, PRISM is flexible enough to accommodate your preferred method in capturing the cost of labor. The objective of capturing the cost of labor is to facilitate PRISM to compute project budget associated with risk mitigation, the cost associated with contingencies, and other costs that affected the project budget. In this workshop, we shall develop PRISM to capture the cost of labor that will later be used to compute the cost of contingencies for all high-impact risks identified in the Risk Register. PRISM tool will be further developed in subsequent workshops when we perform cost budgeting associated with risk mitigation, cost budgeting associated with project liabilities, and cost budgeting associated with project contingencies.

For example, in a software development project, with reference to the "Labor" budget worksheet illustrated above, there are a number of deliverables or work packages with resources assigned to them. Prior to developing program specifications for coding purposes, you will come across one of the work packages called "Develop Design Specification". A design specification is a technical document which refers to the system design associated with the proposed solution. The ownership of this task has been assigned to a resource called the "Solution Architect". Solution Architect is a member of the project team who is responsible for the delivery of this work package. The Solution Architect requires 30 man-days of effort at his daily rate of $900 per day to deliver the Design Specification document. The cost to deliver the work package is 30 x 900 = 27,000.00.

Let's take a look at another example, a work package named "Technical Design Review" requires more than one resources to accomplish the same task. The team comprised of a Project Manager, Solution Architect, Quality Engineer and a PMO Manager. The Project Manager requires 3 man-days of effort to review this document. The Solution Architect, Quality Engineer and PMO Manager require 2 man-days each to perform the same task where their cost varies according to their expertise, roles and responsibilities. A total of 9 man-days of effort is required which cost the project a sum of $21,900.00.

Labor is one of the primary cost drivers of the project budget.

COST OF MATERIAL

Any project will require some sort of tools, machines, or equipment to perform the project activities, we classify them as material. During the planning phase of the project lifecycle, the project team will be working closely with the Project Manager in defining the work packages that formed part of the Project Management plan. After identifying the resources required to execute the work, the Project Manager need to identify the materials that may be required to perform the work. For budgeting purposes, the exact date and time when the materials need to be purchased are not important.

There are many types of equipment that include computer hardware, applications, database, tools, storage, networking devices, and many other materials used in an IT project. It is imperative to capture information associated with all the materials in the project so we can determine the cost of managing this risk should plan contingencies are in place that involved a particular material. There are a number of project documentation that describes the list of equipment used in a project including equipment that is leased for the duration of the project. Project procurement management plan and the project schedule is the ideal place, to begin with for purchases of equipment required for the project. The equipment used in all the phases of a software development lifecycle need to be captured into PRISM.

The development environment consists of application servers, database servers, communication and network equipment are common equipment in any enterprise IT project. These types of equipment will most likely be replicated in the production environment with a much larger scale in configuration i.e., typically in size and performance. The capital cost of these items will be used in a number of project financials, e.g., project contingency reserve involving these types of equipment can be determined when the cost of all materials impacted by the risk event is captured. The process "Define Project Material" will add an important functionality to the PRISM tool to record information on project materials and equipment used in the project. A particular risk event may impact these materials or equipment, there will be some mitigation cost or contingency cost that need to be accounted for and computed as part of the project risk allocations. The calculation for procurement of material is straight forward as depicted above.

MATERIAL

Contractor	GAFM CONSULTING		PRISM Ref:	P1-21-011
Project Name	INTEGRATED BANKING SYSTEMS		Version	V1.0
Subject	PROJECT RISK & PROFITABILITY		Currency	USD
Customer	ABC Banking Corporation			

No.	MATERIAL	DESCRIPTION	Unit Price	Qty	Amount $
1	Development server	3 Development servers, OS, database included	12,000.00	3	36,000.00
2	Test server	3 Test servers, OS, database included	10,000.00	3	30,000.00
3	Production server	3 Production server	15,000.00	3	45,000.00
4	Printers (4 units)	Special high speed color laser printer rent for 6 months	5,000.00	1	5,000.00
5	SAN Storage	Storage 5 TB	35,000.00	2	70,000.00
6	CISCO Network	CISCO networking devices	55,000.00	2	110,000.00
7	Genesis CTI Server	Contact centre computer telephony integration	95,000.00	1	95,000.00
8	Nortel PABX Option 51	PABX system for call centre	250,000.00	1	250,000.00
9					
10					
11					
12					
13					
14					
15					
16					
17					
18					
19					
				MATERIAL	641,000.00

For project execution purposes, a Procurement Management plan that describes details of the purchasing schedule will be produced by the project team. Most likely the central purchasing department will assume full authority in the purchasing of materials and other items required for the project. Some purchases may be going through a tender exercise, while others may just need several quotations, the process is dependent upon the company's procurement policy. Usually, the suppliers have already been identified and pre-qualification exercise conducted during the project initiation phase to save time and cost.

Material is one of the primary cost drivers of the project budget.

COST OF PROFESSIONAL SERVICES

A project may require professional services from vendors, consulting companies, law firms, auditors, quality organizations et cetera which we classify as "service provider". When you purchased computer software, for instance, a CRM application from a vendor, the transaction comprised of several items. The first item is the product license i.e., you get the license to use the product as-is.

SERVICES

Contractor	GAFM CONSULTING		
Project Name	INTEGRATED BANKING SYSTEMS	PRISM Ref.	P1-21-011
Subject	PROJECT RISK & PROFITABILITY	Version	V1.0
Customer	ABC Banking Corporation	Currency	USD

No.	SERVICES	PROVIDER	Amount $
1	CRM Application installation & testing	Simon Technologies	150,000.00
2	CRM Application Customisation	Simon Technologies	85,000.00
3	Voice recording software installation & testing	Duke Systems Inc	50,000.00
4	Project management services	Big Tree Consulting	145,000.00
5	Training and coaching services - Project Management	Prestige Reader	45,000.00
6	Agreement W1-P2100 resources x 5 (expatriates contracted for 12 months)	A-One Manpower	360,000.00
7			
8			
9			
10			
11			
12			
13			
14			
15			
16			
17			
18			
19			
20			
21			
22			
23			
24			
25			
		SERVICES	835,000.00

We shall discuss this further in a chapter titled "Product Licenses". The next item is the application customization effort that is a separate charge. Customization effort is related to the services required to make some minor changes to the CRM software e.g., modification to the standard reports, additional information that need to be added to the screens, integration with some other applications.

A professional service is the services that a contractor or product vendor sells to help a customer manage the specific part of the project development. A resource vendor supply people for specific skills and for a specific duration of time. Vendors that provide these services may have issues in delivering their committed services. There are uncertainties that are beyond the control of the IT vendor, for example, external factors that include regulatory changes, force majeure, and other unknown threats and these threats will directly impact your project implementation. There are many types of IT services and they must be captured into PRISM, this will help the project manager to determine the cost of these services against the overall project budget. Application management and implementation services include the cost of services a vendor provides in delivering a software product, which includes the cost of implementation together with the cost of any customization effort. The primary objective is to determine the budget that needs to be reserved for risk impacting these professional services.

In addition to these, another item is related to the installation services. You will need to pay for the installation of the CRM software on the application server of your choice including configuration of the database server. The software installation services are a chargeable activity. Both customization effort and software installation services are classified as professional services. Software maintenance is also classified as professional services but it will not take effect until the CRM application is fully commissioned. It is a standard practice by international software vendors that issue six months warranty to a commercial application after it is fully installed and commissioned, after which the maintenance services will start. For instance, you purchase the software in January 2016, installed a month later and run live at end of December 2016, the maintenance will only commence on July 1, 2017.

Services is one of the primary cost drivers of the project budget.

There is mitigation cost, contingency cost, the cost associated with liabilities that may be incurred as a result of using the vendor's professional services, and many other types of risk associated with professional services. At the end of this workshop, via "Define Professional Services" process, additional functionality will be added to PRISM that helps to determine the budgeted cost of professional services that need to be allocated for risk management, and most important to the project team is to determine which professional services are expected to cause the highest risk impact to the project budget, scope, and schedule.

COST OF SUBCONTRACTOR SERVICES

Subcontracting is common in any project including FM, IT, and engineering. Subcontracting also includes outsourcing part of the project to third-party providers for the purpose of reducing the risks, or simply because your current team lacks the skills required to execute certain tasks in the project. In information technology, taking advantage of the latest development in cloud computing technology, vendors are offering infrastructure management services to assist organizations in reducing the cost of software development projects. The colossal cost to build a specific development and testing environment for the interest of a group of users in a large enterprise is no longer practical. It is cost-effective to rent the computing resources from a reputable hosting provider that provides most of the IT resources required including database, tools, storage, network, and other services at a fraction of the actual cost. Of course, there are issues like information security that remain to be a challenge but the attractive cost of the services outweighs this risk. Outsourcing services that are commonly subscribed today are Software-as-a-Service, Infrastructure-as-a-

Service, and Platform-as-a-Service. The services provided may be suitable for selective IT projects only where the majority of them are not sensitive to data privacy.

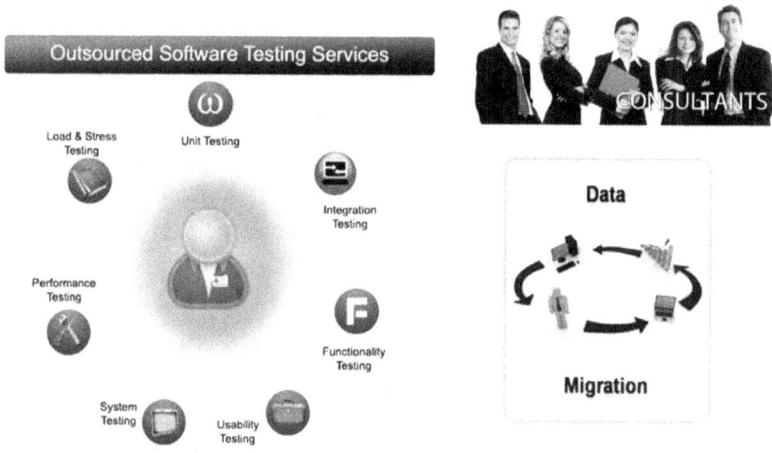

The services may be in high demand in specific industry and least popular in financial services and banking industry where data security and protection are extremely high. While many of these outsourced providers are established, they cannot provide a 99.99% guarantee for the availability of the services, so there is obviously some degree of risks that need to be seriously considered prior to engaging these types of services. In this workshop, via "Define Cloud-computing Risk" process, we will discuss the list of potential threats from the use of these type of services with data security leading the top of this list.

COST OF DATA CONVERSION

There are a number of risks associated with conversion of existing data, where these data are required before the implementation of a new software product. Existing data may not be complete, even if they are complete there are spelling errors, formatting errors, and many other problems with the data. One way to handle this situation is as follows. Determine the state of the data being converted. Is it a straight one to one conversion or is it combining the inputs of multiple files? Will the data need to be "cleaned up" before the new files are constructed, i.e., are there known problems with the existing data that will need to be fixed before the new databases are constructed? What is the risk if the data do not cleanse and updated? We need a data migration plan to handle this situation. The plan must address how to handle these and other situations unique to the project. Support from the client must be negotiated and planned as a part of the work breakdown structure (WBS). This is crucial in situations where data from the old files must be cleansed to create the new databases. The data cleansing exercise is a major effort and poses a major threat to the project during system testing and user acceptance testing. A lot of time needs to be allocated to troubleshoot a software error that is caused by a bad test data. Mitigation plan involving data conversion activity need to be put in place to ensure resources and infrastructure are available to support data conversion process. A contingency plan needs to be defined to ensure that the affected project activities will not be impacted due to unavailability of live data in the production environment. Converting data into the production environment during project transition phase is not only a risky business but costly and time-consuming task. This effort will have to be provided by internal resources however it may be outsourced to an IT vendor depending upon the sensitivities of the data. The technical support for the data conversion effort must be planned and monitored closely. By working closely, the client will have a good idea that what is happening is accurate. Ultimately, the client will have to sign off to validate that the conversion was done correctly. All support activities must be included in the project plan and WBS. The more involved conversion effort will require a greater amount of time and should be planned accordingly. All support activities should be closely tracked, and issues should be raised if any of these activities are not completed in a timely manner. In this workshop, via "Define Conversion Risk" process, we will discuss the list of potential threats from data conversion activity that have a colossal impact on project schedule, budget, and quality.

COST ASSOCIATED WITH PROJECT EXPENSES

Any project will incur expenses, information technology project is no exception. There is a large number of expense items related to project activities so it is not possible to make provisions for each of them in PRISM. The expense data may be extracted from available spreadsheets and loaded into PRISM tool or otherwise, they will be manually captured into PRISM and grouped according to high-level work packages. The project implementation schedule is the ideal place to start since it represents all the activities in delivering a project. Furthermore, the project schedule is commonly developed using a project management tool such as Microsoft Project, hence making the extraction process simpler. How project expenses will be captured depends on the policies of the client organization, and also the project sponsor requirements for tracking and reporting on project performance. Expense item may include meal allowances, rental of equipment, stationaries, accommodation, mileage expenses, et cetera. It is important to capture the complete project expenses in order to obtain accurate reporting on project profitability. Furthermore, the cost of risk contingencies that impacted project expenses will be known. At the end of this workshop, after execution of the "Define Project Expenses" process, additional functionality will be added into PRISM that helps to determine the budgeted cost of project expenses that has been reserved for risk management.

EXPENSES

	Contractor	GAFM CONSULTING		PRISM Ref.	P1-21-011
	Project Name	INTEGRATED BANKING SYSTEMS			
	Subject	PROJECT RISK & PROFITABILITY		Version	V1.0
	Customer	ABC Banking Corporation		Currency	USD

No.	EXPENSE ITEM	WORK PACKAGE	Amount $
1	Staff travel	Flight (10 trips x USD 400)	7,000.00
2	Travelling allowances USD 50 / day	planned 50 days for 10 pax	25,000.00
3	Accommodation	50 days; Hotel (10 x USD 80)	40,000.00
4	Project meals	Meal allowances for project staff	2,000.00
5	Work permit + Agent fee for tax proc.	(USD 1000x5) + (USD 750 x3)	7,250.00
6	Training	Training for 5 pax "testing tool" (USD 500 x 5)	2,500.00
7	Car park	Parking facilities	1,000.00
8	Copier machines	Rental : 2 copier machines for one year	1,200.00
9	Car rental	Rental: 3 cars for 6 months	7,200.00
10	Penetration testing tools	Rental : 3 months for SIT and UAT	5,000.00
11	Stationaries	Paper, Laser printer toners, folders, clips, materials for binding, et cetera	14,000.00
12	Rental of PABX Dev/Test	PABX for Development / Testing - 3 months	50,000.00
13			
14			
15			
16			
17			
18			
19			
20			
21			
		EXPENSES	**162,150.00**

With reference to the example depicted above, work permits issued to expatriates is treated as an expense item although a specific recruitment and placement agency has been contracted by your company to provide the manpower services. This item is not classified as professional services because the services provided by the recruitment agency is not directly contributing toward the development of the project. They merely source for the candidates to be interviewed by the Project Manager. Once selected, the agency will process the work permit and other matters prior to official placement.

Expenses are one of the primary cost drivers of the project budget.

COST OF PRODUCT LICENSES

When you purchased software from Microsoft, you are buying the rights to use the software subject to you agreeing to the product license agreement. The maintenance fee has already been included in the base price for some products while for other corporate or business applications, the vendor will impose a separate annual charge after the expiration of the warranty period. Usually, the warranty period is six months from the date the product is installed and commissioned i.e., used in a production environment.

The tricky part is when you install the product in a development environment, the license to use the product will be activated but the warranty has not started. When you install the product in the Production environment, the warranty kicks in for the duration of 6 months. You are entitled to technical support since the product has already been paid for in full.

Maintenance is not factored in the project operating cost because maintenance services are classified as the company's operation expenditure and not a project capital expenditure. The maintenance fee is calculated based on a certain percentage of the product purchase price which ranges from 10% to 22%. Therefore, we do not include "maintenance services" in a project operating budget.

In any IT project implementation, whether it is infrastructure development, software development, or cloud computing project, there will be a number of product licenses that your client or your company need to purchase. Off-the-shelf accounting software, anti-virus software, Microsoft Office products, and database, all are product licenses that a customer needs to purchase and installed in the development environment, test environment, and the production environment. Although some of these products may be acquired from vendors that provide hosting services i.e., Infrastructure-as-a-Service or Platform-as-a-Service, the cost of engaging these services need to be defined since they have already included the cost of licensing in their service offering.

There are potential threats that may involve these product licenses therefore it is important to identify the cost of these product licenses especially those that are installed in the development environment, and test environment i.e., where the usage of these products falls within the life of the project. At the end of the project lifecycle, after full acceptance of the project outcomes, the risk management process ends, the project will transition to the production environment where the cost and maintenance of these product licenses falls within the jurisdiction of the customer's operation and maintenance.

LICENSES

Contractor	GAFM CONSULTING		PRISM Ref.	P1-21-011
Project Name	INTEGRATED BANKING SYSTEMS			
Subject	PROJECT RISK & PROFITABILITY		Version	V1.0
Customer	ABC Banking Corporation		Currency	USD

No.	PRODUCT LICENSES	third party product	List Price	Discount %	Amount $
1	CRM Application (Vendor: Onyx)	Y	145,000	10%	130,500
2	NICE Voice Recording system (Vendor: Jebsen)	Y	99,000	10%	89,100
3	Microsoft Project	N	35,000	20%	28,000
4	Publishing software - Adobe (Vendor: Bracknel) 10 copies	Y	60,000	10%	54,000
5	GENESIS CTI license (Vendor: Genesis)	Y	240,000	10%	216,000
6	IVR Phone banking Application (Vendor: IntervoiceBright)	Y	220,000	15%	187,000
7	Software version control system	Y	35,000	15%	29,750
8					
9					
10					
11					
12					
13					
14					
15					
16					
17					
18					
			PRODUCT LICENSES		734,350

At the end of this book, through the "Define Product Licenses" process, additional functionality will be added into PRISM that helps to determine the cost of product licenses that has been purchased for the project.

There are 3 categories of liabilities that a Facility Manager is concerned with, they are:

1. Contractual liabilities
2. Financial liabilities
3. Other liabilities

Where a particular liability does not fall into contractual or financial liability categories, we shall park it under "other liabilities".

Project Liabilities

This insurance protects the insured in the event a loss occurs for which the contractor has assumed liability, express or implied, under a written contract. For example, under most FM agreements with a municipality, the contractor agrees to "hold the municipality harmless" for any accidents arising out of the job. Contractual liability insurance would thus protect the contractor from any loss for which the municipality would be liable in connection with the FM.

Penalties will be imposed on Contractors for projects that were delivered later than the agreed schedule. As the Contractor for the e-Banking Systems project, you need to purchase the contractor liability insurance in order to manage the liabilities as a result of late delivery. The amount of the penalty imposed to you is stated in the contract and it has now become a liability to your company.

You will budget 5% of the Project Operating Cost (POC) as the maximum liability for late delivery. In this example, the liability which you can commit is the maximum sum of $136,939. You need to ensure that this sum is sufficient to cover the cost as stipulated in the agreement with the customer. Make provisions at 20% (this quantum varies) of the maximum liability which is the sum of $27,388 to buy insurance for the settlement of the penalty for late delivery.

CONTRACTUAL

	Contractual	POC	Product license	maximum liability	% provision	Amount $
1	Penalty for late delivery	5%		152,939	20%	30,588
2	General damages	10%		305,877	20%	61,175
3	CRM application		10%	13,050	30%	3,915
4	NICE Voice recording system		10%	8,910	30%	2,673
5	IVR Phone banking system		10%	18,700	30%	5,610
6	GENESIS CTI		10%	21,600	30%	6,480
7					SUB-TOTAL	110,441

FINANCIAL

	Financial	POC	contract value	max exposure	% provision	Amount $
1	performance bond		3%	166,500	100%	166,500
2	forex	2%		61,175	5%	3,059
3						
4						
5						
6					SUB-TOTAL	169,559

OTHERS

	Others	details	POC	contract value	Amount $
1	sales commission	sales manager commission		1%	55,500
2	management overhead	management overhead	2%		61,175
3	other liabilities	provisions for other liabilities	1%		30,588
4				SUB-TOTAL	147,263

This is one of the examples of contractual liabilities that an IT vendor has to provide in their project budget. Another measurement of a vendor's performance is based on the delivery of the entire project as committed to the project scope of work. In this situation, the client usually requests a performance bond as a form of assurance that the vendor will deliver the entire project as per the agreed scope, schedule, cost, and quality requirements. The sum of the performance bond shall be mutually agreed upon between the IT vendor and their client which will become the IT vendor's financial liability. The process "Define Project Liabilities" that will be discussed in this workshop will reveal the list of project liabilities in an IT project including software development projects, IT infrastructure projects, and cloud computing-based projects. At the end of this workshop, additional functionality will be added to PRISM that helps to determine the project liabilities that need to be factored into an IT project.

In another case, you are committed to delivering the functionalities as described in the Functional Specification document for the NICE Voice Recording system, however, you foresee potential technical constraints during the planning phase that will impact the delivery of this system. You are fully aware that the customer imposed a penalty of 10% of the purchased price if this system is not delivered according to the specifications. This product was purchased at $130,500 and provisions made at 30% for the purchase of insurance to support this liability.

General damages are monetary recovery in a lawsuit for injuries suffered (such as pain, suffering, inability to perform certain functions) or breach of contract for which there is no exact dollar value which can be calculated. In the context of this project, when dispute arises and the customer won the lawsuit, the contractor is liable to pay for general damages that will be decided by the court. There is no rule of law or a formula to determine the quantum for provisions on general damages. The best approach is to settle the dispute out of court.

FINANCIAL LIABILITIES

Large projects that run into millions of dollars are usually high-risk projects. Obviously, the customer needs some sort of assurance that the contractor can deliver the project within the agreed schedule, within the project scope, and meeting the quality requirements. As a contractor, you are required to provide some sort of a guarantee in the form of a performance bond. Performance bond is usually fixed at 5% of the project contract value however this quantum is subjective. It may be higher or lower subject to negotiations.

Performance bonds: there are two main scenarios the Contractor will have to pay for where performance bonds may be used:

- where the customer requires a performance bond to be issued in its favor by an acceptable surety to cover claims which may arise against the Contractor during the FM phase when, if a default were to occur, it is likely that the Contractor would not be able to meet a claim.

- where the lenders require performance bonds to be issued on behalf of a key Contractor because they are not satisfied with the financial strength of that contractor.

COSTS ASSOCIATED WITH CONTINGENCY RESERVES

The **contingency reserve** is the budget to do the things that may or may not have to be done but that have been identified. This is where the funding for risks that actually take place comes from. When a risk takes place, the project manager authorizes budget to be taken from the contingency budget and placed into the operating budget. Generally, the project manager must approve budget transferred from contingency reserves to operating budgets. The transfer of funds must include any appropriate changes to scope or schedule.

Contingency reserve is the cost or time reserve that is used to manage identified risks or "known-unknown" (known=identified, unknown=risks). Contingency reserve is not a random reserve, it is an estimated reserve based on various risk management techniques, such as Expected Monetary Value (EMV) and the Decision Tree Method.

This reserve is controlled by the project manager. The project manager has full authority to use it whenever any identified risk occurs. The Project Manager can also delegate this authority to the risk owner who will use this reserve at the time of risks occurring. The project manager can be updated on later stages.

A contingency reserve is usually controlled and released within specific guidelines by the project manager when a particular risk occurs. This reserve is usually included in the project's budget.

The contingency plan describes the procedures and processes that would allow the project team to continue to work should its present workplace become unusable or unavailable. What will be the budgeted amount of execution of this contingency plan? Which project objectives will be most likely affected as a result of this risk? Knowing this information will help a project manager to be more proactive in managing risk and also in controlling project cost.

Risk #	Risk Title	Risk Description	Risk Response	Mitigation plan	Contingency plan	Probability	Impact (L/M/H)		Impact on labor/mat/serv/exp/licen	Contingency reserve($)
1	Data Conversion	Data need to be cleanse after performing data conversion because of poor data quality.	ACCEPT: Prepare mitigation plan to address this risk.	Clean data prior to conversion. Employ additional resources to clean the data manually prior to conversion.	Plan for additional 20 man-days on labour. Hire Data Conversion Expert to perform automated data cleansing	70%	H	L	20,000	14,000.0
								M		0.0
								S		0.0
								E	2,000	1,400.0
								P		0.0
2	System Integration testing	System integration testing will require more than two cycle of testing.	ACCEPT: Negotiate with all vendors / suppliers to agree with the anticipated additional time	Perform only critical system integration testing and obtain customer concurrence	Add one more test iteration : estimated 5 days of effort and provide for miscellaneous expenses.	50%	M	L	17,500	8,750.0
								M		0.0
								S		0.0
								E	5,000	2,500.0
								P		0.0
3	User Acceptance Testing	Time allocated for UAT is not sufficient in anticipation of a complex integration component from third party software.	ACCEPT: Negotiate with all vendors / suppliers to agree with the revised UAT schedule	Negotiate UAT schedule.	Extend all contractor services with additional 3 weeks for testing.	50%	M	L	20,000	10,000.0
								M		0.0
								S		0.0
								E		0.0
								P		0.0
4	PABX system for Dev / Test environment	Only 1 PABX for Production Env was purchased, Need to rent a PABX for Dev / Testing purposes to avoid violation of IT security policy.	ACCEPT: Prepare a budget paper to rent this equipment for 3 months.	Request budget $50K	Negotiate with supplier to loan us a smaller PABX if project sponsor decline the requisition. Allocate 100K for purchase if loan is not available	70%	H	L		0.0
								M	145,000	101,500.0
								S		0.0
								E		0.0
								P	9,900	6,930.0

A contingency reserve is usually controlled and released within specific guidelines by the project manager when a particular risk occurs. The alternative plan can be initiated in the situation where risk mitigation plan has been exhausted. Although these types of plans are viewed as plans of last resort, they can be useful in a variety of ways. For example, should a production environment installation be delayed due to unforeseen circumstances, the project team shall allocate an alternate solution in order to allow the project to continue to run within the agreed implementation schedule. In another example, a project team could have a disaster recovery plan in place should a natural disaster, such as a hurricane or earthquake. A contingency reserve is usually included in the project's budget that is parked under a dedicated project contingency reserve account. The contingency reserve is the budgeted cost of executing a contingency plan which is sometimes called an alternative plan. At the end of this workshop, via the "Define Contingency Reserve" process, additional functionality will be added into PRISM that helps to compute the sum of all contingencies that need to be allocated in the project, and also the breakdown of the contingency cost provided for labor, material, services, expenses, and product licenses.

RISK STRATEGIES AND BUDGET ALLOCATION

Perhaps it would be a good idea to review how the budget is allocated for different risk strategies. Risk avoidance is frequently going to cost some budget. The budget that we spend to redesign the project so that the risk is eliminated is budget that will have to be spent regardless of the probability of the risk. The additional work of doing the redesign and adding more expensive parts will be part of the operating budget. No budget needs to be put into the risk reserves if the risk is completely eliminated. If the risk has already been allocated funding in the contingency budget, the increase in the operating budget can be taken from the contingency budget.

Risk acceptance will have budget put into the contingency budget if the risk has been identified. If the risk is an unknown risk and has not been identified, the budget for it will be roughly estimated and become part of the management reserve. If the risk does happen, the budget is taken from the contingency budget or the management reserve and moved into the operating budget when the plan for dealing with the risk is put into place.

Risk mitigation will have budget put into the contingency budget to handle the risk if it occurs. There will also have to be budget put into the operating budget to take care of the cost of the mitigating activities that are being taken for this risk. The mitigation of the risk will reduce either the probability or the impact of the risk, and the contingency budget should therefore be reduced.

Risk transfer requires budget to be put into the operating budget to pay for the additional cost of either subcontracting the risk or buying insurance for it. The budget to do the work for the activity affected, not including the risk cost, was put into the operating budget when the task was created. The cost of the transfer, either the additional cost that the supplier will receive or the cost of the insurance premium, must be added to the operating budget. This budget can be taken from the contingency budget.

The operating budget of the project, sometimes called the performance budget, is the amount of budget needed to do the things that are planned for in the project. This includes all of the work to produce all of the deliverables that were planned for in the project. It is not the total project budget; it includes funding only for the things that are planned for. Subject to limitations in the project policy, this budget can be spent freely by the persons responsible for the tasks of the project as long as the expenditures are following the project plan.

The contingency reserve is the budget to do the things that may or may not have to be done but that have been identified. This is where the funding for risks that actually take place comes from. When a risk takes place, the project manager authorizes budget to be taken from the contingency budget and placed into the operating budget. Generally, the project manager must approve budget transferred from contingency reserves to operating budgets. In larger projects a subproject manager may approve these funds. The transfer of funds must include any appropriate changes to scope or schedule.

The management reserve is budget that is set aside for the risks that have not been identified, the so-called unknown risks. This transfer is made when a risk occurs that has not been identified and budget must be spent to solve the effects of the risk. The use of these funds usually has to be approved by a manager one level above the project manager.

CONTINGENCY RESERVE AND MANAGEMENT RESERVE

The following are a few differences between the contingency reserve and management reserve:

Contingency reserve is used to manage identified risks, while management reserve is used to manage unidentified risks.

Contingency reserve is an estimated figure based on Expected Monetary Value (EMV), or the decision tree method. Management reserve is calculated as some percentage of the cost or duration of the project.

COST OF INFLATION

When you receive a quotation from a vendor, the validity period is 30 days. The vendor cannot guarantee that the cost of goods or services will remain after the expiry of the quotation. When you request a new quotation three months later, the prices have changed.

The cost of inflation on goods or services will cause a negative impact to any project. The rising cost of materials or services will certainly impact the project profitability. How do you control or mitigate this risk? If the project does not require any item from abroad, then your project will be the least impacted by the foreign currency fluctuation. But this is not generally the case. The majority of the projects will need some sort of equipment or products from overseas, and the fact remains that technologically advanced products are not available in one particular country. Most of the foreign suppliers are trading in US dollars, if your currency is weakening against the US Dollar, you will eventually need to spend more to acquire the same product.

Purchasing an item from a local distributor or a value-added reseller will not guarantee that the price of the item will remain fixed unless there was a clause in the sales order form that indicates that the price is fixed regardless of the currency fluctuations. Based on past project experiences, the supplier usually indicates in the terms and conditions of purchase that the pricing will be subject to the prevailing currency exchange rates and the final price inclusive of customs duty will be revealed when the goods have safely arrived into the country.

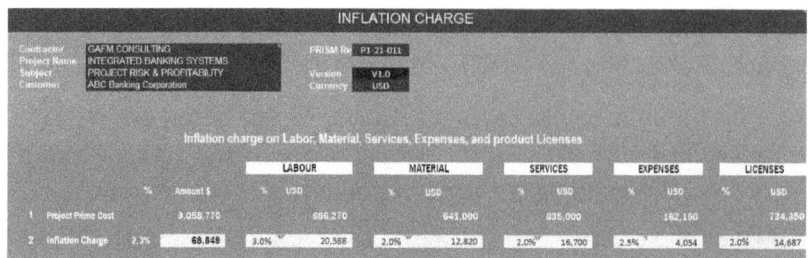

This is mostly the case for imported material or equipment. As a buyer, the inflated cost of these goods or services due to fluctuations in foreign currency need to be accounted for in the project budget. This can be achieved by defining an accurate estimation of the foreign currency exchange rate. The rates for inflation charges need to be defined in cases where human resources are acquired from overseas. The resources are usually booked several months ahead of their required placement however, the actual disbursement will only take place when they have reported for duty. The rates for inflation charges need to be allocated for IT equipment and software product licenses should these are purchased from international vendors. For instance, Oracle database licenses may be quoted in local currency since there is already a local distributor or a direct representative office based in that country that is authorized to transact in the local currency. Different companies apply different policies, products from other vendors may not work the same way as Oracle products. The project manager must be vigilant in the procurement process specifically for products or services from international suppliers. Project expenses too will be subject to inflation charge for staff traveling expenses that are incurred for jobs performed in a foreign country. At the end of this workshop, via "Define Inflation Charge" process, additional functionality will be added into PRISM that helps to determine the rates for inflation charges that need to be allocated for labor, material, services, expenses, and product licenses.

Controlling Cost

Cost Control is the task of overseeing and managing project expenses as well as preparing for potential financial risks. This job is typically the project manager's responsibility with the assistance of a project cost manager. Cost control involves not only managing the budget, but also planning, and preparing for potential risks. During the implementation and execution of projects, procedures for control and record keeping are very important to project managers. In project management, the tool that serves a different purpose in recording different financial transactions to indicate the problems or progress that are associated with the project.

Control costs are defined as processes for monitoring the status of a project in order to update the project costs. This will allow project managers to manage the changes in the cost baseline if present. It is important to take note that there will changes in the cost in any project life cycle. The benefit of the control costs is that it gives project managers a way to determine different variances from the plan, particularly on the cost so that they can take the appropriate corrective action to reduce the risk.

Project management relies on control costs in order to determine the changes in the costs involved in implementing and executing the project. It relies on both inputs and outputs in order to analyze the cost data. The inputs necessary include the project management plan, funding requirements, work performance data and organizational structure. Using this information, project managers can create different outputs such as cost forecast, change request, project management plan updates and other updates concerning the documents and organizational structure.

Control costs require project managers to constantly review the budget as well as other financial information on a regular basis. This will ensure that all costs will be accounted for as well as determine potential cost risk of the project. Simply coming up with a project budget is not enough during the planning session of your project. It is crucial for the entire team to keep a watchful eye on the cost to be always aware of the risks and how to avoid or mitigate them.

Chapter 9 : RISK AND COMPLIANCE

A facilities manager ensures that the organization conducts its business processes in compliance with laws and regulations, professional standards, international standards, and accepted business practices. These professionals perform audits at regular intervals and execute design control systems, advising the management on possible risks that might occur, and organization policies. The major task of a facilities management officer is to uphold the ethical integrity of the organization and also ensure that business activities are conducted using a regulatory framework. These professionals carry out the risk management process by thorough planning of business and implementing the policies within the organization.

Facilities managers are considered to be a vital component of corporate governance. They are also responsible to determine how an organization should be handled and governed. These responsibilities include maintaining good rapport between the stakeholders and adhering to the objectives set by the organization.

The roles and responsibilities of a facilities manager varies depending upon the industry, but typical responsibilities are described below:

- They are accountable for ensuring all the essential guidelines are put in proper place accurately adhering to industry rules and regulations.
- They conduct internal audits and reviews at regular intervals to ensure that compliance procedures are regularly followed.
- They conduct environmental audits adhering to environmental standards.
- The facilities management officer role involves the safety of employees and businesses as well. It's their part of duty to ensure all the tasks are done with higher accuracy.

- They have to ensure that all the employees are thoroughly updated about the organization's policies, regulations, and processes
- They should advise the management regarding the implementation of compliance programs associated with asset maintenance.
- They must adhere to the training and supervising the staff that needs attention to rules and regulations.

FIRE RISK ASSESSMENT

It is important to carry out a fire risk assessment appropriate to the particular workplace. It is also good practice to involve staff in the process, as they may have identified a potential fire risk of which people higher up the organization may not be aware.

The two most important questions to ask are:

- How likely is it for a fire to start in my workplace?
- How easy is it for employees, and other people who may be affected, to escape to a place of safety in the event of a fire?

In larger workplaces, it is good policy to carry out a separate inspection for each significantly different section, area or department. The whole of the work place should be taken into account, including any outdoor areas and any rooms or parts of buildings that are not currently in use. Even if the workplace has been subject to previous approvals by the various enforcing authorities for other safety, licensing or building legislation, you are still required to carry out an assessment of your fire precautions. However, if there has been no significant change in the workplace, for example, in the number of employees or the activities which they undertake, it is unlikely that any significant additional fire precautions will have to be provided. If you do propose to make changes to your fire precautions as a result of carrying out a fire risk assessment, these must not conflict with the controls imposed by other legislation. If in any doubt, you are advised to consult a fire safety officer from your local fire service.

If other employers share your premises, your organization has a responsibility to ensure that they are made aware of any significant risks and any action you have taken to reduce that risk. In addition, you should take all reasonable steps to coordinate your fire safety measures with those of any other employers who may share your workplace.

IDENTIFY FIRE HAZARDS

Potential fire hazards in the workplace will include potential sources of ignition, sources of fuel and any hazards associated with the processes carried out in the workplace. Identify the location of people at significant risk in case of fire This step needs to take into account not only employees, but other people who may be in the premises, such as customers, members of the public, visitors and contractors. The special needs of any disabled staff and visitors must also be considered. There may be parts of the premises where people are more at risk than others.

EVALUATE THE RISKS

This step involves deciding whether existing fire precautions are adequate, or whether improvements are required to remove the hazard or to control the risk. It is necessary to look at any existing fire safety measures provided in terms of:

- the control of ignition and fuel sources
- fire detection and fire warning systems
- means of escape
- means of fighting fire
- maintenance and testing of fire precautions

- fire safety training for employees.

The nature of the risk evaluation will depend very much on the nature of the workplace and the work activities carried out.

RECORD FINDINGS AND ACTION TAKEN

The facilities management officer requires organizations that employ five or more people to record the significant findings of the assessment and any group of employees identified as being especially at risk. There is a legal requirement to provide employees with 'comprehensive and relevant information'. This means telling employees or their representatives about the risk assessment findings, and perhaps making the formal risk assessment report available to them on request.

KEEP ASSESSMENT UNDER REVIEW

It is good practice to carry out an annual review of the workplace to ensure that no new risks have developed as a result of, for example, changes to work processes, machinery, substances or the number of people likely to be present in the workplace. There should also be a reassessment of the workplace if you have carried out alterations or extensions, as they may have affected the fire precautions previously provided.

FIRE RISK ASSESSMENT CHECKLIST

Escape routes

- Are main and emergency stairways protected by self-closing fire doors?
- Is the emergency route clearly sign posted?
- Are there any 'dead end' conditions where escape is possible in one direction only?
- Is all escape routes clear of obstruction?

- Are all exit doors unobstructed externally?
- Are there enough exits?
- Are exit doors free to open at all times (not locked)?
- Are fire doors fitted with 'fire door keep shut' signs, and is this instruction followed?

Fire Defense Equipment

- Is the fire alarm system satisfactory for the risk?
- Will it meet current legal requirements?
- Is the fire alarm, hydrants, fire extinguishers/hose reels, sprinklers and emergency lighting maintained by qualified people? Is maintenance recorded in a logbook?
- Is the fire alarm tested weekly?
- Does the fire alarm have automatic fire detectors in corridors, stairways and risk rooms?
- Are routine checks made to ensure that equipment has not been obscured, moved or damaged?

Work Equipment and Furnishings

- Are all items of portable electrical equipment inspected regularly and fitted with correctly rated fuses?
- Is the wiring of electrical installations inspected periodically by a competent electrical engineer?
- Are the use of extension leads and multipoint adapters kept to a minimum?
- Are flexible electrical leads run in safe places where they will not be easily damaged?
- Is upholstery in good condition?

Cleanliness and Tidiness

- Are staff encouraged to tidy their personal workplaces?
- Are the premises kept clear of combustible waste?
- Are metal bins with closely fitting lids available for waste such as floor sweepings?
- Are separate, clearly labeled containers provided for waste and special hazards, such as flammable liquids, paint rags, and oily rags?
- Are waste containers removed from the building at the end of each working day or more frequently if necessary?
- Is waste disposal put in a safe place which is not accessible to the public?
- Is the burning of waste on site prohibited?
- Are cupboards, lift shafts, spaces under benches, gratings, conveyor belts and similar places kept free from dust and the accumulation of rubbish?
- Are pipes, beams, trusses, ledges, ducting and electrical fittings regularly cleaned?
- Are areas in and around the building kept free from accumulated packaging materials and pallets?
- Are metal lockers provided for employees' clothing?

Storage

- Are fire doors, exits, fire equipment and fire notices kept unobstructed?
- Are storage areas accessible to firefighters?
- Are stack sizes kept as small as possible?
- Are there adequate gangways between stacks?

- Are stacks stable?
- Are stocks of material arranged so that sprinkler heads and fire detectors are not impeded and are the required clearances beneath this equipment maintained?
- Are excessive quantities of stock avoided?
- Is access to storage areas restricted to those who need to be there?
- Are stocks kept well clear of light fixtures and hot service pipes?

Maintenance of Buildings

- Is every point of entry to the site and building secure against intruders?
- After the closedown of operations are all doors, windows, and gates checked and secure?
- Is the building regularly inspected for damage to windows, roof and walls?
- Are the grounds surrounding the premises kept free of combustible vegetation by regular grass cutting and scrub clearance?
- Are all outside contractors supervised while on the premises and their work authorized by 'permit to work' schemes?

Heating and Lighting

- Are there restrictions on using unauthorized heaters?
- Are combustible materials at a safe distance from appliances and flues?

- Is care taken that no materials are left on heaters?
- Are portable heaters securely guarded and placed where they cannot be knocked over or ignite combustibles?
- Are goods kept clear of lighting equipment?

SMOKING

- Is smoking prohibited in all but designated external 'smoking' areas?
- Where smoking is permitted are there enough ashtrays or other disposal facilities?

STAFF TRAINING

- Are new staff instructed in fire procedures and shown the fire escape routes on their first day at work?
- Are fire action notices posted throughout the workplace?
- Are there trained fire marshals?
- Is there a designated fire assembly point?
- Have staff had the opportunity to operate a fire extinguisher?
- Do staff know how to deal with the disabled, the public and visitors in the event of an evacuation?

COMPLIANCE IN ASSOCIATION WITH FACILITIES MANAGEMENT

In recent years, throughout the world we have followed the high level of corruption in various economic sectors. Several companies end up having their image and reputation weakened due to their proven involvement, both at the business level and in the political sphere. The imperative need to know and practice compliance in day-to-day activities arose in the midst of this reality, which affects companies of all sizes and industries. The concept of compliance in relation to facilities management aims to generate value for an organization and ensure its survival.

This practice arises from the great financial impacts caused by factors such as:

- Absence of normative guidelines
- Misalignments to applicable laws
- Lack of adequate preventative tools
- Process management failures
- Operations without a structured information system.

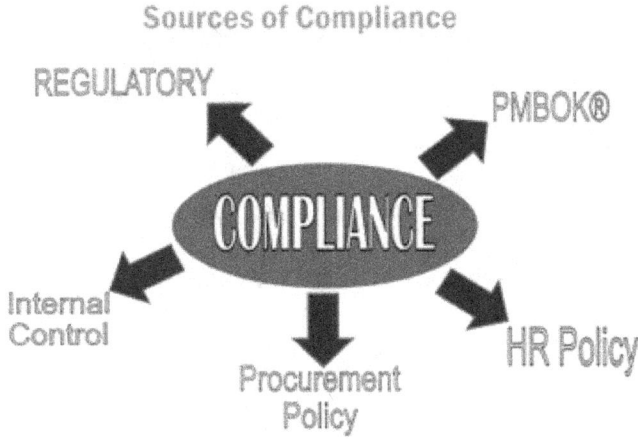

The verb comply means to conform to a rule, which explains much of the concept of the word. The meaning of the word compliance is related to the conduct of a company and its compliance with the rules of regulatory bodies. What is compliance in business, in short? It means to comply with laws and regulations. This concept covers all the policies, rules, internal and external controls to which an organization must conform. When in compliance, an organization's activities will be in full accordance with the rules and laws applied to its processes. Both the company and all its people, including suppliers of interest, need to behave in accordance with the rules of regulatory bodies. In addition, they must ensure faithful compliance with the various internal normative instruments. Only in this way will the company comply with regulations for environment, labor, finance, work safety, operations, accounting, etc.

How Important is Compliance in Facilities Management?

Being able to say that a company is in strategic compliance is by itself a fundamental business strategy. It means that there is transparency and an increasing degree of management maturity. Being in compliance shows that facility managers and teams are in control of the processes and procedures, implemented and executed with effective political, commercial, labor, contractual and regulatory compliance. Not being in compliance means being unnecessarily high risk, which can lead to financial, equity and market losses, among many others. Risk management and compliance are closely linked. It is necessary to reflect and change management styles, adjust the way company information is handled and how people behave on a day-to-day basis, in order to achieve a level of excellence in compliance regardless of the business sector and size of the company.

How To Align Facilities Management with The Concept of Compliance

Now that you know what compliance in business is, check out some tips:

- Use information systems that support monitoring of the company's activities and that conform to compliance processes.
- Have contract management for services and materials that is aligned with the levels of compliance established by the company.
- Strengthen inspection and inspection routines of activities, including those that do not usually have certifications.

- Focus on process compliance at the municipal, state, and federal levels.
- Have an active and updated system of standardization in the company.
- Have internal audit processes focused on the requirements to achieve compliance.
- Have control systems with adequate depth degrees.
- Have structured communication about the normative instruments of the company.

WHAT IS A COMPLIANCE FRAMEWORK?

Formally, a compliance framework is a structured set of guidelines to aggregate, harmonize, and integrate all the compliance requirements that apply to your organization. In practice, a compliance framework lets you take a collection of documents, policy manuals, procedure descriptions, mission statements, regulatory mandates, control documentation and meld those things into one cohesive whole. A compliance framework brings order to the ceaseless stream of regulatory mandates that rain down on a large organization so that when something new comes along, you have a method for integrating that new requirement into your existing approach to compliance. Compliance frameworks are usually tailored to a specific issue. For example, you might follow one framework to guide your anti-graft compliance, another to guide your data privacy compliance, and a third to guide anti-discrimination compliance. Your compliance program would use those frameworks to measure its progress on all three issues.

WHY DO COMPLIANCE FRAMEWORKS EXIST?

Compliance frameworks exist to help compliance officers build a compliance program efficiently. You would miss too many steps, or take certain steps out of ideal order and end up repeating your work, or repeat the same step over and over and waste program resources. Some parts of the enterprise might be managing compliance risk brilliantly, while another part is managing the same risk terribly and you, the compliance officer, might not be aware of the discrepancy. Which could lead to awkward conversations with regulators if you experience a compliance failure, and those regulators start asking about the effectiveness of your compliance program.

Let's remember that all large organizations already have at least some compliance activities happening around their enterprise, and many will even have quite a lot of compliance activity happening. Your job as a compliance officer is to wrestle all that activity into one disciplined program that meets all the regulatory obligations your company has. A compliance framework lets you proceed through that work in a methodical way, so you can reap the most benefit for the least expense of time, resources and your own sanity!

Moreover, compliance frameworks provide a standard that others can use to judge your compliance program. That is, when regulators or the board, or auditors, or business partners ask, "How strong is your compliance program? You can map your program and its activities to what those frameworks require. Those parties can then better understand the program improvements you have already made or the ones you still need to make.

COMPLIANCE WITH COMPANY POLICIES

A policy is a written statement about how your company views certain risks. It can be a simple rule that states what the company's compliance objective is. For example, for anti-bribery, the policy could be something like the one below:

The company is committed to conducting its business in an ethical, honest, and transparent manner. Bribery and corruption are not consistent with our values, and present significant risks to its business. Therefore, employees should never offer, give, solicit, or accept a bribe; whether cash or other inducement to or from any person or company. The company is committed to the prevention, deterrence, and detection of bribery and corruption.

Corporate policies are the backbone of a compliance program. Unto itself, however, a policy usually does little to teach employees or agents and other third parties how to act when faced with a particular temptation or risk. That's where procedures come in.

What are Compliance Procedures?

Procedures provide employees and agents with guidance about how to act under certain circumstances, to ensure that they don't violate corporate policies.

For example, you could require employees to seek approval from the legal or finance department demonstrating a legitimate business purpose before offering to pay travel and lodging expenses for a foreign government official. You could also require prospective agents to complete a due diligence questionnaire, or have employees complete their own due diligence checklists as part of the agent pre-hire process.

A compliance framework will help you understand what procedures you should put into place. A framework can identify which ones make the most sense for your organization, and clarify the work that will be necessary to put those procedures into effect.

What Are Compliance Controls?

Controls, by contrast, are specific checks or gateways intended to prevent improper transactions from happening. They are usually administered by accounting or compliance personnel or, even better, are automated parts of your IT systems to help assure that policies and procedures are not subverted. For example, a control could be something as simple as requiring two authorized signatures on an approval to spend money entertaining a foreign official; or as complex as disallowing any payment to an agent or reseller whose due diligence is not already complete. Another might be to disallow any spending requests at all from employees who have not completed necessary anti-bribery training or policy attestations. All controls aim at the same goal, that is to control and oversight of corporate transactions, so those transactions unfold according to company policy and regulatory obligations.

COMPLIANCE PROCESSES

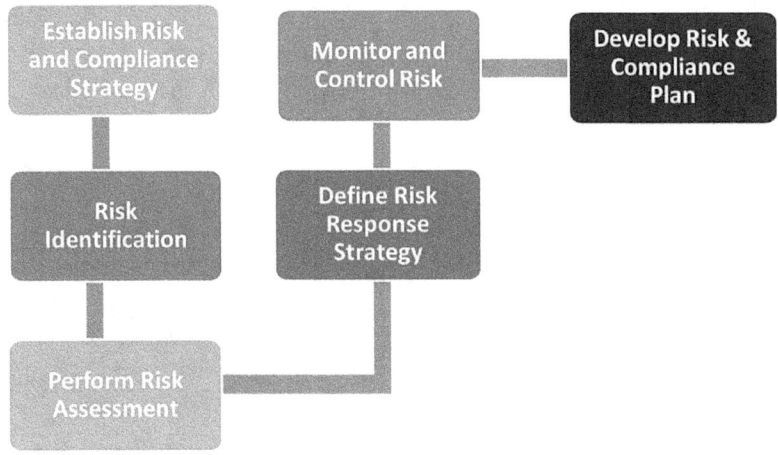

Step #1 Establish Risk and Compliance Strategy

The process **"Establish Risk and Compliance Strategy"** is the first process out of the six processes associated with managing risk and compliance.

In this process, the following topics will be discussed:
- Project risk management
- Importance of risk management and compliance in projects
- Governance structure and stakeholder responsibilities
- Define risk management and compliance strategies

Step #2 Risk Identification

The process "**Risk Identification**" is the second step out of the six-step processes associated with managing risk and compliance.

This step discusses the process for identifying the various risks affecting a project. Risks must be identified clearly so that the true problem is addressed. This process includes identifying risks arising from subcontracting work, risks associated with procurement of goods and services, and risks arising from other sources that impact the outcome of the product or services.

Step #3 Perform Risk Assessment

The process **"Perform Risk Assessment"** is the third step out of the six-step processes associated with managing risk and compliance.

In this step, the various categories of risk including the processes associated with risk management and how they are being applied in the respective phases of the project life cycle shall be discussed.

Associated with this step includes the role of the project organization and stakeholders.

Step #4 Define Risk Response Strategy

The process **"Define Risk Response Strategy"** is the fourth step out of the six-step processes associated with managing risk and compliance.
Risk Response is the process to determine how to deal with the various risks that has been assessed, whether you choose to accept or ignore the risk, avoid the risk completely, reduce the likelihood or impact of the risk if it occurs, or transfer the risk to another party.

Step #5 Monitor and Control Risk

The process **"Monitor and Control Risk"** is the fifth step out of the six-step processes associated with managing risk and compliance.

Monitor and Control Risk is the process of keeping track of the identified risk, monitoring residual risks and identifying new risks, ensuring the execution of risk plans, and evaluating their effectiveness in reducing risk.
This process records risk metrics that are associated with implementing contingency plans.

Step #6 Develop Risk and Compliance Plan

The process **"Develop Risk and Compliance Plan"** is the final step out of the six-step processes associated with managing risk and compliance.

Information gathered from previous processes will be used as input into the development of the organization's Risk Management and Compliance Plan. This document will be reviewed for acceptance by the Executive Committee before it can be applied in the organization.

SPOTTING HAZARDS

Ways of identifying hazards include asking employees or their safety representatives what risks they have noticed; consulting accident and ill-health records, suppliers 'manuals, the trade press, relevant legislation and guidance; or seeking advice from consultants.

Typical hazards to watch for include:

- physical hazards (e.g., poorly guarded machinery, mezzanine floors, slipping/ tripping hazards, vehicles, poor electrical wiring, fire hazards)
- hazardous substances (e.g., chemicals, dust, fumes)
- a hazardous work environment (e.g., noise, poor ventilation, bad lighting, hot or cold workplaces)
- psychological hazards (e.g., stress, long hours, shift work)
- ergonomic hazards (e.g., repetitive work, lifting).

WHO MAY BE HARMED?

Those at risk may be:

- employees (e.g., office, operational and maintenance staff)
- contractors (e.g., cleaners and security guards)
- members of the public and volunteers

- young and inexperienced workers
- new and expectant mothers
- staff with disabilities
- home, lone and mobile workers.

Risks may increase at certain times of day, such as after dark or during busy periods.

CONTROLLING THE RISKS

It is important to consider whether existing precautions:

- meet legal requirements
- comply with industry standards
- represent good practice
- reduce risks as far as reasonably practicable.

If not, an action plan will be necessary, categorizing remaining risks as high, medium or low risk. Priority should go to those measures that will protect the whole workplace. The aim is to eliminate hazards altogether (e.g., by not using a hazardous substance) or, if this is not possible, to control risks, in order of preference, by:

- combating risks at source (e.g., if steps are slippery, treating them is better than displaying a warning sign)
- preventing access to the hazard (e.g., by installing machine guards, using permits to work which restrict access to authorized staff, isolating a dusty area)
- organizing work to reduce exposure to the hazard (e.g., by rearranging work patterns to reduce stress)
- issuing Personal Protection Equipment (PPE)

- providing welfare facilities (e.g., washing facilities to remove contamination).

Taking advantage of technical advances can make work processes safer and more efficient. It is also crucial to provide relevant training and information to staff, and in shared workplaces, to swap information with other firms on site.

RECORDING THE FINDINGS

Generally speaking, organizations with five or more employees must write down their risk assessment. The document can make cross-references to the health and safety policy and other relevant paperwork, rather than repeating everything. An inspector or a union safety representative may ask to see the risk assessment, or it may provide evidence in the event of a personal injury claim.

REVIEWING AND REVISING

Most health and safety legislation require employers to review the risk assessment and revise it as necessary, if it is 'no longer valid or there has been a significant change'. Hazardous substance and asbestos assessments must, however, be reviewed 'regularly', and HSE guidance states that this is good practice for any risk assessment. Significant changes that may make the risk assessment out of date could include bringing in new machines, substances or procedures.

The Management Regulations require risk assessments to be 'suitable and sufficient'. This means:

- allocating appropriate resources
- making the level of detail proportionate to the risk: overcomplicated assessments of simple hazards are not required
- anticipating 'foreseeable' risks

- ensuring that consultants have sufficient understanding of particular work activities
- adapting any 'model' assessment to the actual work situation
- drawing up a timetable for implementing short, medium and long-term controls
- reviewing non-routine activities such as maintenance, cleaning, loading and unloading vehicles, changes in production cycles and emergencies
- reviewing off-site activities, such as home working
- complying with specific regulations; although repeating assessments is not necessary
- addressing what actually happens in the workplace, not what the works manual says should happen.

Chapter 10 :   RELATIONSHIP MANAGEMENT

Customer Relationship Management is a comprehensive approach to creating, maintaining and expanding customer relationships. Let's take a closer look at what this definition implies. First, consider the word "comprehensive." CRM does not belong just to sales and marketing. It is not the sole responsibility of the customer service group. Nor is it the brainchild of the information technology team. While any one of these areas may be the internal champion for CRM in your organization, in point of fact, CRM must be a way of doing business that touches all areas. When CRM is delegated to one area of an organization, such as IT, customer relationships will suffer. Likewise, when an area is left out of CRM planning, the organization puts at risk the very customer relationships it seeks to maintain.

CRM is the most important component in facilities management. If you want to repeat business from your existing customers, the only way is to ensure your company maintain a good relationship with the customers. The quality of services provided added to strong communications across all levels of employees in the client organization is imperative to ensure repeat business for a long time.

The second keyword in our definition is "approach." An approach is "a way of treating or dealing with something." CRM is a way of thinking about and dealing with customer relationships. We might also use the word strategy here because, done well, CRM involves a clear plan. In fact, we believe that your CRM strategy can actually serve as a benchmark for every other strategy in your organization. Any organizational strategy that doesn't serve to create, maintain, or expand relationships with your target customers doesn't serve the organization.

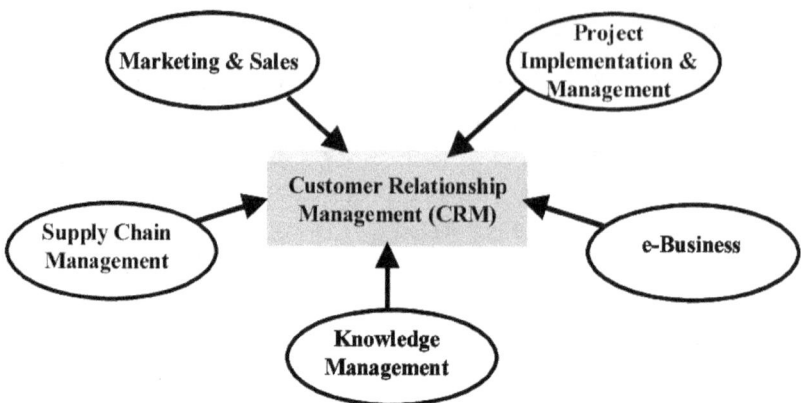

The strategy sets the direction for your organization. And any strategy that gets in the way of customer relationships is going to send the organization in the wrong direction. You can also consider this from a department or area level. Just as the larger organization has strategies and plans for shareholder management, logistics, marketing, and the like, your department or area has its own set of strategies for employee retention, productivity, scheduling, and the like. Each of these strategies must support managing customer relationships. Sounds too logical to need to be mentioned. Yet it is all too easy to forget.

For example, in times of extremely low unemployment, how tempting is it to keep a less-than-ideal employee just to have a more comfortable headcount? Or, consider the situation all too familiar to call center environments, where the pressure to keep calls short goes head-to-head with taking the time necessary to create a positive customer experience.

Are you a manager whose area doesn't deal with external customers? This part of the definition still applies. First, you and your team support and add value to the individuals in your organization who do come into direct contact with customers. Again and again, the research has proven that external customer satisfaction is directly proportional to employee satisfaction. That means that the quality of support given to internal customers predicts the quality of support that is given to external customers.

Second, consider your internal customers as advocates for your department or area. For you and your team, CRM is about growing advocates and finding new ways to add value. Finally, what do we mean by "customer relationships" in today's economy, where we do business with individuals and organizations whom we may never meet, may never want to meet, much less know in a person-to-person sense? CRM is about creating the feel of high touch in a high-tech environment. Consider the success of Amazon.com. Both of us are frequent customers and neither of us has ever spoken to a human being during one of our service interactions. Yet, we each have a sense of relationship with Amazon. Why? Because the CRM tools that support Amazon's customer relationship strategy allow Amazon to:

- Add value to customer transactions by identifying related items with their "customers who bought this book also bought" feature, in much the same way that a retail clerk might suggest related items to complete a sale.
- Reinforce a sense of relationship by recognizing repeat shoppers and targeting them with thank you'd ranging from thermal coffee cups to one-cent stamps to ease the transition to new postal rates.

In short, customers want to do business with organizations that understand what they want and need. Wherever you are in your organization, CRM is about managing relationships more effectively so you can drive down costs while at the same time increasing the viability of your product and service offerings.

CRM Strategy

The overall strategy for delivering services to customers can be described by the term 'relationship management". When organizations operate in a service-oriented economy, relationship management is an important requirement for managers. It embraces marketing services, developing a unique way of providing the service (service concept), working to an operating strategy and having a service delivery system. Organizations need to recognize that their employees are the most valuable asset in their fight for advantage in any highly competitive marketplace. They may be the first point of contact that a customer has with an organization's core product or service. It is vital, therefore, that this contact is optimized by removing any distractions from the employee serving that customer.

Support services are conventionally categorized as overheads, but can be given priority according to the role they play in support of key business activities. For example, direct services support front-line activities, whereas administrative overheads support internal customers. They can also be rationalized as essential and non-essential services. Basic services are delivered to service levels agreed with customers clients and representatives of end users. Their delivery should add value to the services being offered. Planning for support services must start by identifying the services needed to support the enterprise/operation. In addition, the user's requirements and the dimensions of service quality for a customer focused internal organization, together with the techniques for negotiating, evaluating and monitoring service performance, all need to be identified. In commerce or industry, general services support the production and delivery of a product or service. In the public sector they are delivered either direct to the community or to support direct services and the organization itself.

Developing customer relationship in facilities management can be an extremely complex process, as there may be a multitude of internal and external customers. The juxtaposition of the needs of those working in the building and external customers using the building, together with statutory requirements and wider social and environmental issues, can create conflicting needs which have to be resolved. A building performance-type approach can be used to derive criteria against which the service may be appraised. This entails determining user requirements and identifying the needs that can be met from current resources. Service and functional requirements are derived from this base and the performance specified. It is against this that potential providers can offer to deliver services and justify their performance. Service appraisal will include evaluation by the provider and surveys of user response and satisfaction. Service quality is determined by the capability, approach and credibility of the provider. These are the main components of service quality and need to be identified and managed.

A developing facilities management role is defined by its relationship with the core business and its success is measured by the support it provides in achieving key business objectives. Hence, facilities are not only strategically planned but have a clear relationship between their development and operation and the business need. In the climate in which business operates, the primary organizational need is for greater adaptability. Included in this is the need to anticipate differential rates of change, accommodate expansion and contraction and enable a rapid response to business opportunities. For this, management decisions need to be taken in real-time. Established organizations in the public and private sectors in the United States, which have traditionally emphasized stability, status and position, are undergoing extensive programmed of change and corporate restructuring. Resulting pressures lead to a reduced headcount and closely controlled costs. Hitherto, morale has been linked to security, routine and stability in job tasks, but future demands are likely to focus on independence and creativity. As organizations developed, they take a different form with different working patterns. The indications are that, as management gurus suggest, these 'new organizations' are flatter without formal hierarchies, with decentralization and devolution of responsibilities, and with an end to long-term, secure careers for corporate managers. Organizations tend to evolve towards this new model as they seek to improve competitiveness. Successful companies and public bodies cultivate corporate cultures that emphasize innovation and change. They organize around work processes rather than around formal hierarchies and prescribed functions. They build around relationships of trust.

Many organizations distinguish between the roles of purchaser and provider and adopt the contract as a basis for service delivery, which means that they can release management time by using consultants and contractors. The issues of third-party facilities management, outsourcing options and contracting out are central, and standards of performance and responsibilities for meeting them are defined by service-level agreements and contracts. The value added by business services, particularly those involved with facilities management, is created by designing relationships that respond to these conditions and provide effective support for the achievement of business objectives. These relationships release management time and concentrate resources on the core business activities. Appropriate relationships are established within which people are empowered and decisions about the use of facilities are taken closer to the customers. The level of responsibility and degree of autonomy provided to the facilities enterprise, and the commitment and encouragement it receives to improve quality, determines the value that can be added.

CRM-Driven Strategy

One of our clients, a resort, has developed the following mission, and service strategy.

Mission: To create an innovative and unique experience for families, groups, and individuals in this fun, relaxed environment, through entertaining, educational programs from a knowledgeable staff interested in making every experience a happy, treasured one.

Service Strategy

- We will create relationships by understanding the unique expectations of each of our guests and equipping our staff to meet those expectations.

- We will maintain relationships by constantly identifying opportunities to enhance our guests' experience and further our mission, including partnering with other local attractions.

- We will expand relationships by rewarding customers who help us grow our business by recommending our resort to new customers and visiting us frequently.

Outsourcing Relationship

Surveys have consistently shown that companies are, in general, dissatisfied with the overall results of their outsourcing agreements. So how can you make the outsourcing relationship one of value, providing ongoing benefits to your business?

To have an outsourcing relationship that works, it is important to consider the supplier as a source of value that needs to be constantly realigned if the contract is to succeed. Levels of service need to be continuously improved if they are to result in long-term relationships. This calls for flexibility, which starts in the planning stage and should be the result of candid communication, frankness and a willing approach to working with the aim of creating a 'win–win' situation. With a good plan, there should be flexibility to meet new opportunities and redefine the relationship on an ongoing basis. That means measuring the value and rewarding the supplier on their ability to deliver that value. Then the bar can be raised continually and the relationships can be moved and aligned with business objectives.

Defining added value

Decide early on how to define added value. Look for one or more of the following:

- the ability of the supplier to come up with initiatives that reshape the relationship to meet ongoing objectives
- the ability and willingness of the supplier to set and meet concrete and measurable service levels
- the ability of the supplier to commit to and meet specific financial targets.

Clear channels of communication need to be mapped out which encourages the supplier to be proactive and bring ideas to the strategy of your business. The supplier should also be rewarded for ideas and revenue opportunities, with rewards reflecting the benefits brought by the implementation of ideas.

Good Communication

Ideally, the relationship should start with each organization appointing an informed and empowered point of contact, to act as contract administrator. These two individuals are responsible for making the relationship work, as opposed to the site managers who will oversee the day-to-day running of the function on site. This is an important first step in implementing a successful outsourcing relationship. Other factors which help to build and sustain the partnership include a strong management team; a dedicated account manager; a good working relationship between management on both sides; a consistent communication chain; a single point of contact, possibly the administrator to resolve queries and remove duplication; and a database of written communication between parties to track commitments.

Trust is essential in developing a successful outsourcing relationship, and communications need to be based on this. An outsourcing contractor should be instrumental in the client's success. Therefore, they need to have access to the information they need. It is necessary to drive home what the business is all about; highlight objectives; be frank in disclosing issues facing the company or its industry, both short and long term; give the supplier the tools they need to achieve or maintain status as an industry leader; and be clear about the roles in the relationship.

COORDINATING STANDARDS AND BUDGETS

Relationships need to be developed at multiple levels throughout the organizations involved, to create the trust and understanding required for long-term success. Both parties need to coordinate standards, such as protocols and business processes, and perform joint budgeting exercises to understand the key cost driver information inherent in the other's infrastructure. In addition, there needs to be qualitative information associated with the reliability and performance of the outsourced services.

ANTICIPATING PROBLEMS

Most problems arise because the client underestimates the services, they will require the supplier to undertake. In addition, the client often fails to say up front what work is in the scope of the contract and what work is additional. This can lead to a misunderstanding of responsibilities. For example, the manager of a client's data center is frequently retained in-house to help manage the supplier. That manager is familiar with the way the center used to be operated in the past but, of course, the supplier may choose to do things differently. This may cause problems all around. As this example shows, most management problems are not actually 'people' problems, more a result of a lack of clarity over how key objectives are to be implemented. This highlights the importance of the contract. Without a suitable contract, the two parties enter their 'marriage' and may go into the honeymoon stage, where everyone is enthusiastic and focused on the objectives of the agreement and the potential benefits that are to follow. At this stage, everyone talks frequently, gets involved with fine-tuning objectives, works enthusiastically towards service levels and has great expectations. However, too often time erodes this initial flurry of excitement and a sense of anticlimax develops which can lead to exasperation. At this point, communication breaks down, key people leave, the original mission is lost, the client and supplier forget original objectives, and frustrations grow. Ensuring that the contract is clearly defined, that flexibility is built into it, and that there is constant scope for communication and assessment and reassessment of the tasks and responsibilities in hand will help to prevent misunderstandings and frustrations.

CRM Success Factors

While clear intention fuels the power of CRM, there are several other success factors to consider. We will focus on five of the most important here. Organizations that implement CRM with a strong return on investment share these characteristics.

Strong internal partnerships around the CRM strategy. We said earlier that CRM is a way of doing business that touches all areas of your organization. This means that you and your management peers need to form strong internal partnerships around CRM. If you and your organization are early on the road to CRM implementation, now is the time to bring your CRM needs to the table, and to be open to listening to the CRM needs of other areas. You may find that you have requirements that are, at least potentially, in conflict. Resist the temptation to go to war for what you need. If your organization has gone off the partnership road with CRM, then now is the time to come back together and rebuild the partnership with the area that is currently championing CRM. Let them know that you appreciate what they have done. Let them know what data you have to offer and help them understand how you plan to use the data you request from them.

Employees at all levels and all areas accurately collect information for the CRM system. Employees are most likely to comply appropriately with your CRM system when they understand what information is to be captured and why it is important. They are also more likely to trust and use CRM data when they know how and why it was collected.

STAKEHOLDERS

Organizations, whether publicly listed (commercial), not-for-profit, or government bodies must deliver the strategies and requirements defined in their mission and vision, charter or articles of incorporation. The FM leadership team is accountable for the delivery of these strategies. Success is not necessarily or universally about delivering bottom-line success. It can be defined in other ways depending on the corporate, legal, legislative or social responsibilities and requirements of the organization. Success is bound up in how well the organization conducts its activities, whether strategic, operational or tactical, to meet these requirements.

Success is measured in part by reports of financial compliance, and in part by other less tangible aspects such as meeting the expectations of its stakeholders (the public, government, shareholders, customers, employees, lobby groups or voters).

The organization needs to focus on different sets of activities for the successful delivery of its vision, mission and business strategy.

WHO CAN BE STAKEHOLDERS?

Stakeholders may be groups or individuals who supply critical resources, or place something of value at risk through their investment of funds, career or time in pursuit of the organization's business strategies or goals. Alternatively, stakeholders may be groups or individuals opposed to the organization or some aspect of its activities. Stakeholders are defined as 'individuals or groups who will be impacted by, or can influence the success or failure of an organization's activities.

Stakeholders in tourism are individuals or organizations that have an interest in the tourism industry. They can be directly involved in the industry, such as tourism businesses or government agencies, or they can be indirectly involved, such as local communities or environmental groups.

The Facilities Management (FM) function often has a longer list of stakeholders than any other part of the organization. This may include staff, product suppliers, and service providers, building occupants, senior managers, investors, neighbors, unions, landlords, auditors and regulatory bodies.

WHAT IS AT STAKE?

By definition, a stakeholder has a stake in the activity. This stake may be:

- an interest;
- rights (legal or moral);
- ownership;
- contribution in the form of knowledge or support.

INTEREST

An interest is a circumstance in which a person or group will be affected by a decision, action or outcome. An example of interest is to consider a public event, such as a major sporting contest, being conducted in a residential area. For the time that event is running and also over the time it takes to set it up and take it down, the residents will have an interest in that event, even if they are not interested in that particular sport.

RIGHTS

Rights can be either legal or moral rights. Legal rights cover the legal claim of a group or individual to be treated in a certain way or to have a particular right protected. Legal rights are usually enshrined in a country's legislation; examples include privacy laws and occupational health and safety.

Moral rights cover moral issues that may affect large groups of people or natural phenomena, such as environmental, heritage or social issues. Social issues may extend to speaking on behalf of countries or individuals who cannot speak for themselves or defend themselves and encompass both the activists and the 'victims. Moral rights are usually not covered by the legislation. It is moral rights such as the ones described here that organizations may address in corporate social responsibility (CSR) activities.

OWNERSHIP

Most stakeholders will have an interest, many will have rights. Many individuals will also have a stake of ownership, such as:

- a worker's right to earn their living from their knowledge;
- shareholders' ownership of a portion of an organization's assets;

- intellectual property resulting from the exploitation of an idea;
- legal title to an asset or a property.

KNOWLEDGE

A team member or employee who applies experience or knowledge to the production of an asset for an organization will be making a contribution to the organization's activity. This knowledge is important to the organization's success, but as discussed earlier, the employee or team member will be impacted by the success or failure of the activity.

CONTRIBUTION

The contribution that a stakeholder may make to the activity falls into the following categories:

- Allocation of resources - this can be people or materials.
- Provision of funds - either the initial approval or ongoing assurance of continued funding.
- Knowledge or experience essential for the successful achievement of the objectives of the activity.

Knowledge of the stake that a stakeholder may have in the success or failure of the activity will be important information for managing the relationship between the work of the activity and stakeholders. To clarify the nature of this relationship and to further develop the concept of 'who can be stakeholders?' and 'why are they important?' it is important to discuss the various assumptions, frameworks and definitions of the nature of any relationship between an organization, its activities and its stakeholders.

Chapter 11 :   LEADERSHIP MANAGEMENT

Leadership is a management approach in which leaders help set strategic goals for the organization while motivating individuals within the group to successfully carry out assignments in service to those goals. It entails directing and coordinating individuals within an organization to achieve its goals or mission. Whether you're seeking to achieve higher levels of management or leadership, or you've reached a ceiling at your workplace and are looking for the next step, organizational leadership might be the right next step for you.

Leadership jobs are impacted by the company one works for and the actual position. Despite being an important skill, "organizational leader" is not the actual title most often given. Organizational leaders are initially termed "high potential" employees. As they move up the ranks in a company, business, or nonprofit, they then enter organizational leadership roles with managerial and director-level titles such as dean, provost, general counsel, chief financial officer, etc. The actual day-to-day tasks and responsibilities of an organizational leader include managing and motivating a team, utilizing a problem-solving mindset to address any problems that may arise, setting team goals and coordinating with other departments as broader organizational goals are being pursued.

The importance of organizational leaders is bolstering teamwork, promoting cooperation, and setting reasonable goals by making the most of the unique skill set found in their team. A possible example of organizational leadership is managing a team project researching how a company can improve its website search engine optimization (SEO). In this scenario, the leader figure will help coordinate individuals and their strengths, encourage inclusivity, and ensure a plan is set with each person taking on the responsibilities to see it through.

Some important traits for organizational leaders include:
- Problem-solving and decision making

- Clear communication and good listening
- Inclusivity and fostering a safe environment for employees
- Goal oriented
- Respect and courtesy
- Creative in utilizing the team's strengths

Leaders inspire others to act by setting good examples. Their drive and perseverance spur others on. Leaders strive to be the best they can be not to compete with others. In fact, a leader's job is to help others make their best contribution toward a shared goal. Leaders motivate others through mutual trust. The leader must trust in his or her teammates' abilities and willingness to pursue a goal. At the same time, the team must trust in their leader's ability and willingness to provide needed support. This mutual trust is essential in building a team that will be successful in reaching its goal. In today's workplace, you need to develop leadership skills to build and direct teams to get work done. Although some leadership qualities are inborn, many of the skills necessary for good leadership can be learned. In this book, we discuss ways of interacting with others that will help you lead them to success. Topics include:

- Motivating others
- Giving and taking criticism
- Organizing a project
- Delegating responsibility
- Monitoring a team's progress
- Learning leadership skills on the job

What Makes A Good Leader?

Although there are different styles of leadership, all effective leaders share certain characteristics. These are qualities that can be learned and improved upon over time.

Communication Skills

They communicate clearly. Managing a group, especially in the workplace, starts with good communication. Whether writing an e-mail or providing face-to-face employee feedback, good leaders say what they mean and mean what they say. They're not passive-aggressive, nor do they shy away from addressing challenges in a direct manner.

Passionate

They're passionate about their work. Many good leaders love what they do, and they're not afraid to show it. Of course, you can still be a good leader even if your professional and personal interests aren't a perfect match. Think about what you enjoy most in your work, and develop your enthusiasm around that you even may find that you're managing yourself into greater workplace satisfaction.

Unpopular

They don't care about being popular. In fact, if your first concern is whether everyone likes you, you may be less effective. Whether it's giving tough criticism or pointing out a practice you believe is unethical, learning how to be a good leader means getting comfortable doing or saying things that are best for your team and your organization, even if it makes you temporarily unpopular

Think Positive

They're positive and encouraging. Good leaders are uplifting. They praise employees for a job well done, taking time to coach and train if there are lapses in performance. In good times and bad, good leaders bring out the best in their employees by encouraging them to be their very best.

Connection

They build relationships. The ability to form productive connections is a key quality of a good leader. Strong managers aren't threatened by others. Instead of guarding their territory, they're constantly building bridges with others. A good leader knows the value of mutually beneficial relationships, and actively seeks them out.

Lead by Example

They lead by example. The best managers know that an essential part of what makes a good leader is setting the right example. From putting in extra hours on a major project to treating others with respect and kindness, good leaders show they're ready and willing to do anything they'd ask of their employees.

Innovation

Leaders must be able to do the job, but ability alone is not enough. True leadership requires a willingness to be bold, to consider unusual approaches to problems, to do more than just follow tried-and-true methods. Leaders are self-confident and have no need to put others down to feel good about themselves. They are willing to stand up for their ideas and debate them with others. This kind of intellectual competition is characteristic of a good leader.

Respect for Others

Balancing competition with respect may be difficult for young employees who think the way to get ahead is to outshine their coworkers. But neither workers nor supervisors like or respect leaders who think only of themselves. Above all, leadership requires the ability to get along with others in a variety of situations. For example, if you are class president, you won't be able to accomplish much if you begin to think too highly of yourself. Classmates you snub are not likely to volunteer to help with prom decorations. Likewise, if you are an assistant manager and ignore your coworkers until you need something, you will not always get the results you want.

Courteousness

Treat others as you would like to be treated. The workplace is still primarily a place where people interact. The social skills we have been practicing all our lives are important in business, too. In meetings, leaders must clearly communicate their ideas to team members, while still being open to suggestions from others. Corbis talking, avoiding sarcastic comments, and controlling emotional outbursts. Sarcasm and temper tantrums are not acceptable in a social setting and even less so in the workplace. Being in a supervisory position doesn't give you the right to be discourteous.

Sensitivity

Although they are important qualities, courtesy and agreeableness are not the only qualities of a good leader. He or she must also be sensitive to the feelings and needs of others. These needs are not always clearly expressed. Sometimes people do not even know what they want or need. Talented leaders are able to "read" the people around them and adjust their own behavior accordingly.

The aim of good management is to provide services to the community in an appropriate, efficient, equitable, and sustainable manner. This can only be achieved if key resources for service provision, including human resources, finances, hardware and process aspects of care delivery are brought together at the point of service delivery and are carefully synchronized. This chapter first discusses good management and leadership in general, then outlines relevant considerations for managing relations with patients and the district team, as well as finances and hardware and management schedules.

MANAGERS AND LEADERS

In the leadership development industry, there is a lot of confusion about the relationship between leadership and management. Many people use the terms interchangeably. Others see them as separate, but give different reasons why.

MANAGER	VS	LEADER
• gives direction		• asks questions
• has subordinates		• has followers
• holds authority		• is motivational
• tells you what		• shows you how
• has good ideas		• actions good ideas
• reacts to change		• creates change
• tries to be a hero		• makes hereos
• exercises power		• develops power

Most dictionaries suggest leadership and management are quite similar in guiding or controlling a group of people to achieve a goal. Most web articles suggest that leadership and management are different, but offer contradictory reasons, such as: leadership inspires, management plans; leaders praise, managers find fault; leaders ask questions, managers give directions; etc. However, the qualities often ascribed to leadership can also apply to managers. There can be good and bad leaders, and there can be good and bad managers.

Management and leadership are important for the delivery of good health services. Although the two are similar in some respects, they may involve different types of outlooks, skills, and behaviors. Good managers should strive to be good leaders and good leaders, need management skills to be effective.

Leaders will have a vision of what can be achieved and then communicate this to others and evolve strategies for realizing the vision. They motivate people and are able to negotiate for resources and other support to achieve their goals.

Managers ensure that the available resources are well organized and applied to produce the best results. In the resource-constrained and difficult environments of many low to middle-income countries, a manager must also be a leader to achieve optimum results.

What are the attributes of a good leader?

Leaders often (but not necessarily always):

- have a sense of mission;
- are charismatic;
- are able to influence people to work together for a common cause;
- are decisive;
- use creative problem solving to promote better care and a positive working environment

LEADERSHIP AND MANAGEMENT

There is an essential difference between leadership and management which is captured in these definitions:

- Leadership is setting a new direction or vision for a group that they follow, i.e.: a leader is the spearhead for that new direction.

- Management controls or directs people/resources in a group according to principles or values that have been established.

There is much more to these definitions than may at first appear. Albert Einstein said that everything should be made as simple as possible but no simpler. However, it is an oversimplification to think that leaders lead and followers follow, because the relationship between leadership, management, and followers is a complex one. Also, leadership and management are often part of the same role because there is a continual adjustment of the direction (leadership) and controlling resources to achieve that direction (management). We can see the difference more clearly by looking at some examples of leadership without management, and management without leadership.

LEADERSHIP WITHOUT MANAGEMENT

The difference between leadership and management can be illustrated by considering instances when there is one without the other. Leadership without management sets a direction or vision that others follow, without considering how the new direction is going to be achieved. Other people then have to work hard in the trail that is left behind, picking up the pieces and making it work.

You can see an example of this in Lord of the Rings. At the council of Elrond, there is an argument about how they should proceed. Frodo Baggins rescues the council from the conflict by taking responsibility for destroying the ring. He sets a direction but has no idea how to go about it. During the quest, most of the management of the group comes from others, particularly Gandalf and Aragorn.

There can be leaders who don't manage in the workplace. For example, an entrepreneur might grow a business by networking, building relationships, and generating ideas for new products. However, he/she might also rely on a deputy e.g., a factory manager to ensure the right staff are recruited, products or services are produced, and the business is delivered.

MANAGEMENT WITHOUT LEADERSHIP

Management without leadership controls resources to maintain the status quo or ensure things happen according to already-established plans. For example, a sports referee manages opposing teams to ensure they keep within the rules of the game. However, a referee does not usually provide "leadership" because there is no new change, no new direction. Also, what is often referred to as "participative management" can be a very effective form of leadership. In this approach, a new direction may seem to emerge from the group rather than the leader. However, the leader has facilitated that new direction whilst also engendering ownership within the group i.e., it is an advanced form of leadership.

SYMBOLIC LEADERSHIP

Sometimes, an individual may act as a figurehead for change and be viewed as a leader even though he/she hasn't set any new direction. This can arise when a group sets a direction of its own accord, and needs a spearhead in order to express it.

In prison, Nelson Mandela was an example of symbolic leadership. Although his ability to take action was limited, he continued to grow in power and influence (as the symbolic leader for the anti-apartheid movement). This power came from the mass movement, from the group that are nominally viewed as the followers. Following his release from prison, he demonstrated actual leadership by leading South Africa into a process of reconciliation rather than retribution. This illustrates the complexity of the relationship between leaders, followers, and context. A leader's power often comes from the followers. For example, in democratic government, leaders are elected because of the direction they offer e.g., for economic growth or social development. However, if they subsequently pursue a direction that is different from the expectations of the electorate, they may lose the next election, or even provoke civil unrest beforehand.

LEADERSHIP STYLES

There are many different types of leadership (or management) style. Different situations, groups, or cultures, may require the use of different styles in order to set a direction or ensure that it is followed.

BEING INNOVATIVE

As leadership involves setting a new visionary direction e.g., JFK setting the goal of putting a man on the moon. As management involves producing creative ideas to ensure the vision is realized e.g., coming up with ideas that enabled Apollo 13 to return safely to earth.

PARTICIPATIVE MANAGEMENT

As leadership involves facilitating a new direction through team discussion. As management involves winning the commitment of a team to a defined goal. Everyone has their own preferred set of leadership styles. One aspect of becoming an effective is to build greater awareness of those styles, learning how to harness them productively, and mitigating natural weaknesses.

LEADERSHIP MANAGEMENT

We are committed to the development of good leadership because no facilities management team can function successfully without it. It is our observation that it is too often lacking. There are other leadership books available. In this chapter, we concentrate on those aspects of leadership considered unique to facility management.

Successful Facility Managers should have the following leadership skills:

- serves at least two constituencies; the external, which is business-oriented and normally political; and the internal, with a results-oriented, technical orientation. He or she must bridge these needs and demands.
- is an activist if facilities are to be recognized as important, and if they are to be managed correctly?
- integrates both diverse technical functions and a diverse workforce to work as a team to accomplish the mission.
- hires well, uses the loose-rein technique, evaluates through agreed-upon metrics, and manages by walking around.
- sets the tone for quality service.
- simultaneously prepares for the future and reacts to today's crisis.
- FM leader must be reactive without being a reactionary.

There is no lack of excellent books on management and leadership and it is not our intention to advocate for one theory over another. Our approach is based on our long service in the profession and our observation of facility management over the past thirty years. At the same time, it is obvious that the composition, expectations, and quality of the facility management workforce have changed. Work itself has changed, the profession must change, and we must change as well. Because facility management is still considered only an afterthought by the management team, facility managers today must become much more proactive business leaders.

Facility Managers must know the business they support, know their own business, run the department like a business, and be able to speak the language of business. How business-like the facility manager is will largely determine how he is viewed outside the department, particularly by senior management. Each organization has its business language and we need to be able to speak in the same language as the decision-makers. Because the Facility Manager is managing technical staff, the facility manager must also be comfortable with the technical aspects of the job. Each of us also needs to be comfortable with quantitative analysis, specifically using numbers to measure operational effectiveness and efficiency. Unfortunately, too many facility managers, probably due to their education, tend to overemphasize their role as technical managers. No one person can expect to be an expert in all FM functions. Therefore, it is important for the facility manager to manage from a customer service perspective and strengthen their knowledge and skills as a business leader. The variety of required FM skills is another reason that we have always favored having a mixed workforce of staff, contractors, and consultants. You can hire specialized expertise to perform the technical duties. Facility managers and key staff employees should be devoted to the leadership and management of the facility's function.

There is always a danger in stating that a certain type of leader of a particular management style will be successful in a given environment or position. However, there are certain leadership traits that are more likely to lead to success. For instance, successful facility managers should possess good management skills, be knowledgeable about facilities, and be comfortable managing experts in design, engineering, technology, finance, law, food service, security, etc. In addition, a good facility manager must be capable of simultaneously handling problems that require immediate resolution and those that are long-range. The facility manager deals with questions for which there are no absolute answers and often that is emotionally charged. He understands his employee base (including contractors) and their needs, as well as the advocates for building services. Some responses will require rapid reaction as well as strategic insight. He needs the ability to allocate shortages as well as resources.

From the discussion above, leading the facility management organization may seem impossible because it is so diverse and the demands are so great. The diversity of functions, the level of activity, the active interest of employees in their work environment (the social status inherent in the allocation of office space, for example), and the recurring lack of adequate resources make the facility manager highly visible. Systems and standards must handle 90-95 percent of the problems, but the facility manager must be personally available and visible to do the following:

- Tend to the other five to ten per cent of the problems.
- Handle exceptions to standards and policies.
- Promote the department as a concerned, cost-conscious service provider and business advisor.

- Reinforce and motivate subordinates.

Because facility management is so diverse, the leader will never be knowledgeable in every aspect of FM. That means he must have a system to produce expert advice at an appropriate time and the wisdom and judgment to sort through often conflicting opinions to decide on a course of action.

As a facility manager, you must be a persuasive advocate for your department. You must know how to exercise the formal and informal chain of authority and communication lines, both internal and external. Your relationship with other key leaders and staff is particularly critical to the department. You must be not only an effective informal communicator but a skilled writer and presenter. You need to develop skills in presenting metrics and building information graphically since most of your audience does not have experience with things such as floor plans and building system metrics.

Since so many decisions involve major expenditures of funds, facility managers are expected to be able to make sophisticated economic arguments. While the number crunching can be done by staff, they must understand the context and methodology of net present value analyses, cost-benefit ratios, payback periods, return on investment, and other financial calculations.

ORGANIZATIONAL GOVERNANCE

The key ingredients to project management are people, processes, and technology. Technology is a tool, while processes provide a structure and path for managing and carrying out the project. The success of a project, however, is often determined by the various project stakeholders, as well as who is (or who is not) on the project team. In this chapter, we will discuss the human resources of project management. The area of project human resource management entails:

- organizational planning
- staff acquisition
- team development.

Project Organization

Key project management committees that are responsible for project delivery and implementation

ORGANIZATION PLANNING

Organization planning focuses on the roles, responsibilities, and relationships among the project stakeholders. These individuals or groups can be internal or external to the project. Moreover, organizational planning involves creating a project structure that will support the project processes and stakeholders so that the project is carried out efficiently and effectively.

STAFF ACQUISITION

Staff acquisition includes staffing the project with the best available human resources. Effective staffing involves having policies, procedures, and practices to guide the recruitment of appropriately skilled and experienced staff. Moreover, it may include negotiating for staff from other functional areas within the organization.

TEAM DEVELOPMENT

Team development involves creating an environment to develop and support the individual team members and the team itself.

This chapter will expand upon these three subjects and integrate several relatively recent concepts for understanding the governance structure in project management. Three primary organizational structure: the functional, project, and matrix will be described. In addition, the various opportunities and challenges for projects conducted under each structure will be discussed. As an Engineering Manager or project team member, it is important to understand an organization's structure since this will determine authorities, roles, responsibilities, communication channels, and availability of resources.

Nothing can be achieved without team effort

In Project Management, the project team carries out the work needed to complete the project.

Once the project team is in place, it is important that the project team learn from each other and from past project experiences. Thus, the idea of learning cycles will be introduced as a tool for team learning and for capturing lessons learned that can be documented, stored, and retrieved using a knowledge management system

Project Stakeholders

Stakeholders are individuals, groups, or even organizations that have a stake, or claim, in the project's outcome. Often, we think of stakeholders as only those individuals or groups having an interest in the successful outcome of a project, but the sad truth is that there are many who can gain from a project's failure. While the formal organization tells us a little about the stakeholders and what their interests may be, the informal organization paints a much more interesting picture.

Budget Management

Engineering Manager must be capable to prepare the project budget. All businesses have a responsibility to the monies they are allotted, have earned, and have acquired through donations. In project management, the work completed within a project must be measured for value and accounted for. The budget the organization has set for the project must be guarded. Ultimately, the success of the project should generate an increase in funds, productivity, or efficiency for the sponsoring organization.

Project Resources

Engineering Manager must be organized. How much time has been wasted looking for documentation, contracts, or permits? How much money has been lost due to disorganization? How many projects have failed because the Engineering Manager did not keep and maintain accurate records? Organization is a methodical approach to storing and retrieving information, as it is needed. Organization does not require a spotless desk, thousands of labeled file folders, or archives of every project-related document. Organization requires thorough, fast, and reliable access to project data.

Team Leadership

Managing a project team is different than leading a project team. It has been said that you manage things, but lead people. In project management, you must create a relationship between the project team members and yourself to excite, motivate, and inspire the workers to move toward the strategy and vision of the project deliverable.

People Management

People management requires several soft skills, including those that can lead to open and honest communication as well as improved employee experience. Each of these skills can better help you interact with your employees and perform organizational tasks.

Here are eight essential people management skills to incorporate into your workplace:

1. Empowering employees
2. Active listening
3. Conflict-resolution
4. Flexibility
5. Patience
6. Clear communication
7. Trust
8. Organization

Empowering Employees

Empowering your employees helps them develop new skills and be more productive. It's important to train new employees well and give them the knowledge and resources they need to perform assigned tasks and continue learning on their own.

Other important aspects of empowering employees include:
- Offering constructive feedback to encourage skill-building
- Being available for questions or additional training
- Allowing them to adjust workflow or standard processes if it improves their productivity
- Encouraging them to take additional skill-building courses and learning opportunities
- Supporting them on or managing challenging projects

ACTIVE LISTENING

Active listening is the practice of listening to the speaker to fully understand their perspective, question or concern before responding. Active listeners remove distractions, maintain eye contact and offer verbal or non-verbal cues to indicate their engagement and understanding. When an employee comes to you with a question or issue, use nonverbal cues such as nodding to demonstrate your engagement while they're speaking. Respond thoughtfully by repeating a summary of your understanding of their message.

If you have understood, you can then ask follow-up questions to learn more about what they need. You can also express that you empathize with their experience to further assure them you understand and respect them. These active listening techniques lead to quality people management that promotes positive interactions in the workplace.

CONFLICT-RESOLUTION

Good conflict-resolution skills can help address interpersonal challenges. You can analyze the situation and identify what the causes of the conflict might be. If there's a miscommunication or differing opinions, you can mediate between opposing parties and help them make a compromise or reach a collective understanding. After mediation, monitor the situation to ensure the conflict is fully resolved and to prevent it from occurring again.

FLEXIBILITY

Knowing when to be flexible and when to more firmly direct employees is an important aspect of effective people management. You can demonstrate flexibility in your management style by accommodating individual employee needs such as adjustable schedules or remote work options—and allowing employees to adjust their individual workflow so they can be as productive as possible. You should assess the results of the employee's process to ensure its efficiency and to help them revise the process if it can be optimized. For example, if one of your employees prefers to complete related tasks in batches while another employee moves back and forth between different tasks, analyze each employee's results. If both employees are their most productive using their respective processes, then you can encourage them to continue using and improving their systems. You may even ask them to demonstrate their individual processes to other employees to optimize the entire team's workflow. If an employee seems to be struggling with personalizing their process, you can coach them through the standard steps, and help them discover what works best for them.

PATIENCE

Patience is an important people management skill that uses kindness, respect and empathy while helping others overcome obstacles. You can use patience when training new employees, teaching new processes, handling conflicts or solving problems. When employees can trust their managers to be patient, they are more likely to ask for clarification to ensure they understand directions and to increase the quality of their work. For example, if an employee continues asking questions about a single process, you should continue to guide them while trying new ways to better communicate your message. Consider providing multiple examples that clarify and demonstrate your instructions, or combine typed instructions with visual diagrams if possible.

CLEAR COMMUNICATION

Communication is a necessary people management skill that enables team members to work together in solving problems, brainstorming new ideas and adapting to new changes. Your ability to clearly communicate with your coworkers can help you be a better team member. Practice effective communication by using clear and simple language so every recipient understands your message. Consider revising the way you give your message to avoid common barriers, such as too much information at one time or inaccessible terms. Allow your employees to ask clarifying questions, and directly confirm that each member of your team understands the information so there is no miscommunication.

TRUST

Trust means believing that you can rely on someone's abilities, assistance or advice when you need it most. Building trust helps your team work together more efficiently and productively. Teams should be able to trust that their leader supports them and believes in their hard work. Leaders should be able to trust that their team can complete tasks correctly and on time. You can build trust by reliably performing your tasks and demonstrating technical skills when employees ask for help. You can also promote trust when you provide constructive feedback that helps team members improve their skills and work quality.

ORGANIZATION

Managing a team involves handling several different ongoing tasks simultaneously. Being organized is an important people management skill that helps you track and maintain your team's productivity. Signs of effective organization include:

- Promptly responding to emails, approval requests and questions
- Keeping a calendar to actively track deadlines
- Running meetings that efficiently discuss information
- Properly assigning tasks to team members
- See your instant resume report on Indeed
- Get recommendations for your resume in minutes

HOW TO DEVELOP YOUR PEOPLE MANAGEMENT SKILLS

If you can demonstrate your people management skills, you can become a stronger candidate for future leadership roles. Identifying your strengths and areas for improvement can help you decide which distinct skills to grow. Consider using these strategies to develop specific people management skills:

Choose individual skills to focus on: People management is a broad skill set. Select a specific skill from the list above, such as conflict resolution, and learn more about the skill, its benefits and how to apply it in the workplace. Enroll in professional development courses: Some companies offer their own management training programs while others may sponsor employees to take professional development courses elsewhere. You can find courses online or through an educational institution. Find a mentor or business coach: Specialized or targeted attention is a great way to develop people management skills quickly. Mentors and business coaches can give you personalized feedback and specific, actionable strategies. Ask other managers for feedback or advice: Ask your manager or supervisor for advice on how to develop your people management skills and potential leadership opportunities where you can demonstrate and practice those skills.

What Is Team Management?

Team management is a manager or organization's ability to lead a group of people in accomplishing a task or common goal. Effective team management involves supporting, communicating with and uplifting team members so they perform to the best of their abilities and continue to grow as professionals. Precisely what constitutes effective team management, however, may differ depending on the work environment and the people. Some managers do well with an authoritative approach, while other managers prefer to manage their teams in a more casual way. Some team members may also respond differently to certain management styles. Understanding your own leadership style and what works best with your team is an important part of team management.

Why Is Team Management Important?

Team management is important for a number of reasons within the workplace:

- It promotes a unified approach to leadership within a company or team, especially when team building is implemented.
- It makes it easier to solve problems through the implementation of negotiating and critical thinking.
- It encourages open communication between managers and team members and emphasizes good communication skills and active listening.
- It ensures managers and team members are working toward a common goal that has been clearly defined.

It helps managers clearly outline the roles and expectations for their team members. Understanding the importance of team management and working to develop your team management skills can help you be the most effective leader possible. The more effective you're at managing your team, the more successful your team will be within the workplace.

EXAMPLES OF EFFECTIVE TEAM MANAGEMENT SKILLS

Effective team managers tend to share certain skills, attitudes and tactics. Although good management involves more than merely applying a list of tried-and-tested methods and approaches, you may benefit from considering practices that have worked well for other managers over the years. If you're new in management or wish to grow your management skills, here are a few ways you can hone your skills as a team leader as well as real-life examples within the workplace.

FOCUS ON SERVING RATHER THAN MANAGING

Although it may seem counter-intuitive, effective managers focus on serving rather than managing their teams. As a manager, you should at all times have the best interests of your team members in mind and should strive to assist and support them in achieving both individual and team goals. In addition, a good manager leads through actions, as opposed to merely giving orders and delegating tasks. If you want your team to act professionally and deliver excellent work, you should act accordingly and set an example.

Example: A team member has phoned to say she is ill and not coming into work. Instead of adding all of her outstanding tasks to the workload of other team members, you offer to complete some of the tasks yourself.

Don't always assume you're right

If you want to be a good manager, you have to be open to continuously learning. While as a manager you may occupy a more senior position than the team members you manage, you should keep an open mind as to what your employees can teach you on a daily basis. Apart from learning from your team, you should also ensure that you stay up-to-date with the latest trends and developments and invest in your own ongoing professional development.

Example: During a meeting with your team, you give your opinion about a technical issue that one of your clients is experiencing. One of your senior technicians responds to your analysis with a different point of view. Instead of immediately assuming your viewpoint is correct, you listen attentively to what he has to say and then have a constructive discussion on the matter.

Make transparency a priority

A transparent workplace can help employees feel more connected and encourage creativity and accountability. Practicing transparency through open and consistent communication allows your team members to feel a sense of respect which is important for overall job satisfaction and productivity. This can also help your team members have more confidence when it comes to contributing ideas and solutions to the workplace, which can ultimately benefit everyone involved.

Example: Rather than distributing team tasks on an individual basis, use a project management system to assign and display tasks and overall goals for a particular project. When team members can clearly see their roles in a project and know exactly what their responsibilities are, they are more likely to hold themselves accountable for producing quality work.

SET BOUNDARIES

Although you want to treat your team with kindness and respect, it is also important to set boundaries and assert your authority at times. Team members should know that your job is to ensure their work gets done efficiently and that, when necessary, you will take disciplinary action. There should be a very clear understanding of responsibilities and roles within the workspace to discourage team members from challenging unclear boundaries.

Example: A client has informed you that one of your technicians has not been attending to the necessary maintenance tasks on a regular basis as per their service agreement. Rather than sending an email to let your technician know they need to update the maintenance tasks, you meet with them in person to clearly outline your expectations and discuss the employee's recent unsatisfactory performance. By meeting in person, you show your team member that you take their performance seriously and that not following through on work assignments will not be tolerated.

PROVIDE A POSITIVE WORKSPACE

Although the business world is a serious place that often involves profit margins, risk assessments and performance evaluations, studies have shown that a bit of humor and light-heartedness in the office can have a remarkably positive effect on productivity. If possible, organize fun work outings or liven up the office environment with some plants and bright colors. Even if you just bring a bunch of flowers to work or tell a joke every now and then, this can brighten your team's day and foster a culture of happiness within the workspace.

Example: The morale in the office is a bit low after losing a big account. You decide to lighten up the mood by hiring a mobile massage therapist to give everyone a shoulder and neck massage. When everyone is a bit more relaxed you sit them down with doughnuts and coffee to discuss lessons learned and how the team can improve on service delivery in the future.

EMPHASIZE CONSTANT AND EFFECTIVE COMMUNICATION WITHIN THE WORKPLACE

One of the most important aspects of effective management is communication. As a manager, you should provide your team with all the relevant information at all times as well as encourage feedback from your employees. As effective communication starts with attentive listening, you should set an example to your team members by really listening to them and considering their opinions and input. You should also strive to foster a work environment where team members have the freedom to express themselves in a polite and respectful manner. Constructive and positive communication does, however, not always involve talking in person. There is an array of social media apps available today through which co-workers can stay in touch with each other and exchange ideas.

Example: You realize there is a lack of communication in the office, which is negatively affecting service delivery. To address this issue, you call a meeting with team members where you discuss processes and where the breakdown in communication is taking place. To assist team members, you provide them with a mobile application on their phones where they can input the necessary updates when they are working outside of the office space.

ENCOURAGE AND NURTURE YOUR TEAM'S GROWTH

As a manager, you should support and nurture your team. Your staff should know you have their personal development and best interests at heart and that you're supportive of their goals and dreams. This means that you should always be on the lookout for ways to develop and enrich your team, such as providing them with opportunities to attend workshops and conferences and stay up-to-date through training and certification. Apart from encouraging your workers to continuously expand their knowledge, you can also nurture and motivate them through positive feedback for good work or improvement in performance. However, you should also provide constructive criticism at times, as this can assist team members in their professional development.

Example: An exciting conference is taking place which involves new technology. Although only senior engineers and management typically attend conferences, you have a talented junior engineer in your team who can benefit from going to the conference. You decide to raise this matter in the next management meeting and request that they allow the junior engineer to attend.

BE OPEN TO CHANGE

To be an effective manager you need to be open to change. This involves adapting your management style when necessary and realizing that different team members may have different approaches and ways of doing things. Be open to trying new technologies and to changing your typical method of management when it no longer produces the desired outcomes.

POSITIVE WAYS TO LEAD BY EXAMPLE IN THE WORKPLACE

A workplace can benefit from having influential leaders in place to guide employees. As a leader, your team looks to you for inspiration, encouragement and direction. You can provide this by leading by example and building a culture of trust and accountability. Leading by example means guiding others through your behaviors and inspiring them to do the same as you. It is a leadership style servant leadership where you model the behavior you want to see in your team.

When you lead by example, you provide a path to direct others so that everyone works toward a goal with the same purpose. A leader makes it natural for people to feel like they want to do the best for the organization they work for. Leading by example can accomplish this and create a workplace filled with trust, confidence and purpose.

BENEFITS OF LEADING BY EXAMPLE IN THE WORKPLACE

Many benefits come from leading by example whether you're an executive or a junior associate. The benefits of having someone or multiple people in the workplace who led by example include:

MORE RESPECT AND TRUST

Someone who leads by example can expect to receive respect from their superiors, people who work alongside them and their employees. They are able to:

- Inspire confidence in others
- Understand the workplace and how everyone works together

- Stick to their word and actively seek solutions to problems
- Form a workplace culture that celebrates everyone's skill set
- Involve every member of the team in projects or important decisions

Higher productivity

When you lead by example, your team will soon follow, working just as hard and accomplishing just as much as you to do their part for the organization. They will strive to make their team proud and not let anyone down by performing below their abilities.

Loyal employees

Leading by example inspires those around you to enjoy being part of the team and a company employee. They want to enjoy the people they work with, including their leader. Satisfied employees have lower absenteeism, are more positive, contribute more to discussions, volunteer to take on more projects or help a coworker.

Commitment to the organization

When there is positive leadership, employees are generally more committed to the company. They strive to help achieve its goals, develop a team mentality and work to support the company's mission, purpose and values. When a leader leads by example and works alongside their team, they inspire others to do the same.

BENCHMARK STANDARDS

A leader's actions set the standard for behavior in the workplace. How you act can determine how team members respond. For example, if you're always on time for meetings, your team will be more likely to do the same. On the other hand, if you don't communicate with your employees, you may notice the workplace becomes siloed and non-collaborative.

Chapter 12 :   COMMUNICATION SKILLS

Communication Skills is the most important skills across any profession

ELECTRONIC COMMUNICATION

There are many forms of electronic communication today, you can communicate via X (formerly known as Twitter), WhatsApp, e-mail, Skype, short messaging service, Telegram, and many other chat applications.

Electronic communication places new demands on language that leads to interesting variations in written language use. Hailed as a powerful educational resource, the electronic communication medium has not only revolutionized the composing process but has also been found to encourage participation in writing activity.

One reason for this is that e-mail and online chats provide a non-threatening atmosphere in which writers feel less inhibited about expressing themselves, encouraging even timid students who usually refuse to speak in face-to-face discussions to actively participate in online chats. Another reason is that the Web provides an arena for writers to present their work to a real and larger audience that extends beyond classroom and school boundaries. When students realize that they are going to put their work on the Web for readers in the real world, they are motivated to write. The electronic communication medium has been found to increase collaborative writing activities. There are mixed views on whether it has a similar effect on the quantity and quality of writing done by individual students.

Because the electronic communication medium reduces the intimidation factor and offers attractive features, it improves students' attitudes towards writing and practicing the target language and encourages students to produce more text. The quality of all relationships is formed and maintained much more through non-verbal communication than through words, which play a relatively minor part. Becoming skilled in reading and interpreting non-verbal behavior is essential to enhancing effectiveness in all relationships and in helping patients. Learning about our own non-verbal behavior, and using that knowledge to influence how we relate to others will help us to see below the surface and to be more useful and successful in everything we do. Physical, and non-verbal elements of the environment also contribute significantly to the messages that patients receive and to their reactions to healthcare. Blindness to non-verbal behavior is almost complete blindness to the meaning and complexity of all communication, of who other people really are and what they are communicating or trying to conceal.

Communication skills are abilities you use when giving and receiving different kinds of information. While these skills may be a regular part of your day-to-day work life, communicating in a clear, effective and efficient way is an extremely special and useful skill. Learning from great communicators around you and actively practicing ways to improve your communications over time will certainly support your efforts to achieve various personal and professional goals. Communication skills involve listening, speaking, observing and empathizing. It is also helpful to understand the differences in how to communicate through face-to-face interactions, phone conversations and digital communications, like email and social media.

There are four main types of communication you might use on a daily basis, including:

- Verbal: Communicating by way of a spoken language.

- Nonverbal: Communicating by way of body language, facial expressions and vocalics.

- Written: Communicating by way of written language, symbols and numbers.

- Visual: Communication by way of photography, art, drawings, sketches, charts and graphs.

E-mail Communication

Electronic Mail or e-mail is a system of electronic correspondence by which users send and receive messages over a network of computer and telecommunication links. The message may consist of short notes and greetings, or extensive text files plus graphics and photographic images, video clips or sound. Thus, e-mail is an 'electronic past office'. It lets people communicate even in the absence of the receiver at the other end. It means that you can send e-mail message at any time or whenever you want. The person, to whom you have sent the message, can read the same whenever he wants. Thus, the sender and the receiver don't have to connect themselves at the same time to communicate that particular message.

Advantages of E-Mail

- It permits sending to and receiving messages from others having e-mail address.
- It transmits the message almost immediately. Thus, its speed is very fast.
- It does not require the presence of the receiver of the message at the other end. The message is delivered into his mailbox and it can be checked by the receiver by opening his mailbox at any time.
- It directly reaches the concerned individual's electronic mailbox.
- It ensures a higher degree of secrecy of the message.

- It is a very cheap medium of communication. Hard copy letters and memorandums can often be replaced by electronic mail.
- Message can be sent at any time, day or night, eliminating problems brought about by differences in time zone.
- Identical messages can be sent to many people simultaneously.

E-Mail Etiquettes

- Respond to an e-mail within 24 hours.
- For convenience of receiver, provide clearly worded subject lines for all messages.
- Use short paragraph for gaining reader's attention.
- Be complete and concise.
- Use upper and lower-case letters for clarity purposes.
- Inappropriate and unpleasant words must be avoided.
- Avoid adding many attachments to your message.
- Always apply personal name if your mail system allows it.
- Re-read and proof read the message before sending.
- Use grammar checker before sending.

If you have access to your boss's e-mail account, I would suggest you regularly read the e-mails, even if they deal with them themselves. It is always useful to be well informed and to have a broad picture of what they are doing.

Remember to put a heading in the subject in your e-mail. Everyone gets so much e-mail and may scan their in-box for ones they feel they need to read urgently, so make the heading something that will entice them to open it and read it. They may use also the subject heading to file their e-mails by. It is important to remember that if you pick up an e-mail to reply to it, you need to change the subject heading if you are emailing about a different subject. E-mails are easy to send but so difficult to retrieve (if at all), and when writing them you should carefully consider the tone and message conveyed. They must be professional, with correct grammar and spelling. You must also make sure they are sent to the correct recipients, with everyone copied in who should be. It is important not to type in capital letters as this is considered to be shouting on e-mail. Also, the human eye finds it easier to read small letters than capitals. If you want to do headings you can make them bold.

Be careful when sending group e-mails that you do not give away people's e-mail addresses against their wishes. You should use blind copy (bcc) to keep the e-mail addresses of each recipient private. Be careful of how you word e-mails and how they read think about how it will come across to the recipient. If you are angry about something don't send off an e-mail in haste: think about it, draft it and go back to it later when you have calmed down; change it or delete it if necessary, and remember it is sometimes better to pick up a phone or meet face to face.

E-mails that are quite curt, short and to the point are sometimes perceived as coming from someone who is abrupt or arrogant. They can irritate some people even though you may be doing it this way because of lack of time. You should write an e-mail, then read it from the reader's point of view imagining how the wording could be interpreted. Messages should always have a greeting at the beginning and be signed off at the end. It is a good idea to use 'signatures', which may include a farewell greeting such as 'kind regards and your full contact details to help the recipients should they want to call you. Similarly, people do not want to receive long e-mails that ramble on but rather ones that are to the point. If it is necessary to give lots of information, this should be attached as a word document rather than in the e-mail itself. Be very careful with sending confidential information in emails as they can be forwarded on and can be read by the company if the authorities so wish. Consider whether it would be better to post or deliver highly confidential material by hand.

Also be aware of your company's e-mail etiquette. Use your personal e-mail address for personal e-mails rather than clogging up the company's inbox with your personal correspondence. Be careful not to use work time for your personal concerns.

COMMUNICATING EFFECTIVELY IN THE WORKPLACE

While there are several communication skills you will use in different scenarios, there are a few ways you can be an effective communicator at work.

Clear and Concise

Making your message as easy to consume as possible reduces the chance of misunderstandings, speeds up projects and helps others quickly understand your goals. Instead of speaking in long, detailed sentences, practice reducing your message down to its core meaning. While providing context is helpful, it is best to give the most necessary information when trying to communicate your idea, instruction or message.

Empathy

Understanding your colleague's feelings, ideas and goals can help you when communicating with them. For example, you might need help from other departments to get a project started. If they are not willing to help or have concerns, practicing empathy can help you position your message in a way that addresses their apprehension.

Assertive

At times, it is necessary to be assertive to reach your goals whether you are asking for a raise, seeking project opportunities or resisting an idea you don't think will be beneficial. While presenting with confidence is an important part of the workplace, you should always be respectful in conversation. Keeping an even tone and providing sound reasons for your assertions will help others be receptive to your thoughts.

Calm and Consistent

When there is a disagreement or conflict, it can be easy to bring emotion into your communications. It is important to remain calm when communicating with others in the workplace. Be aware of your body language by not crossing your arms or rolling your eyes. Maintaining consistent body language and keeping an even tone of voice can help you reach a conclusion peacefully and productively.

ANSWERING THE PHONE

Answer the phone with a smile on your face. The smile can be 'heard' and you will sound happy and pleasant. If you are extremely busy and getting stressed with your work, take a deep breath before you answer the phone to calm you down and make you sound normal and not anxious. Answer the phone promptly don't let it ring more than three times before you answer it. Set yourself a daily challenge to attempt to answer the phone on the first ring so that callers are not kept holding on the line for longer than is necessary, they will appreciate not having their time wasted. This helps exceed expectations when you are consistent. Always be polite, helpful and proactive when dealing with phone calls. Whenever you can, go that extra mile to help the caller or client it always pays off and sometimes it gets back to your boss how helpful you have been. It improves the perception of the company and client relationships as well as your own reputation and relationships.

Always try to help the callers when they ask for your boss. You will often be quite capable of dealing with the call yourself and it is amazing how many times all the caller wants is some information that you can provide. Find out as much information as possible and if appropriate make notes of the call, then inform your boss as soon as possible and get back to the caller. Callers do not always realize that you can do a lot more than just an answering machine so you have to ask probing questions.

COMMUNICATING WITH DIFFERENT CULTURES

Often, we can see the reason behind our own cultural ways and habits, but others may not see them in the same way. The habits, words and gestures of people from different cultures may seem odd and confusing to us. We are increasingly working across cultures and we should be aware and respectful of each other's norms and differing etiquette. If your boss visits another country, research any cultural differences for that country to make sure the boss does not offend anyone. The ritual of shaking hands is especially important and, particularly for women, the dress code. It is a good idea to provide translations of some basic greeting words 'hello, how are you', 'thank you', 'goodbye' and so on. If possible, when planning to do business in other countries it is advisable to try to spend a day or two there beforehand to do some 'on the ground' research. If time affords then suggest this to your boss and schedule it in the diary. Some countries take a much more direct and focused approach than others, while some will require 'small talk' and relationship building before doing business.

Working with different cultures means that there will be a need for clarity in the communications we make and we should watch and listen and learn from others. However, it is worth remembering that respect, openness and courtesy are common to all cultures. Never assume that others think the same. Even people in the same culture may be brought up in a different environment, which makes them differ from each other. Observe people before you do or say anything that may cause misunderstanding or offend another person. Be careful with the English language as it can cause confusion. The meanings of words and phrases may vary in different English-speaking countries such as the UK, Australia, South Africa and the United States.

Body language also means different things in different countries. The common English and American 'thumbs up' (well done) gesture, for example, would be offensive in some countries. Making eye contact, showing the sole of your foot, personal space, sitting down before the other person, reading a business card, and presenting an object with your left hand all these gestures and behaviors can convey very different impressions. Be warned and watch and listen and learn.

WRITTEN COMMUNICATION

Written communication is best suited when the communicator and the receiver are beyond the oral communication medium. The executives in all organizations can maintain effective inter-departmental and intra-departmental connections through messages in written words. The process of communication involves sending a message in written words. Written communication covers all kinds of subject matter like notices, memorandums, reports, financial statements, business letters, etc. This type of communication simply means a process of reducing messages into writing which is extensively used in organizations. Formal communication must always be in writing such as rules, orders, manuals, policy matters etc.

The systematic filing of written communication is one of the important aspects of communication. Filing along with indexing is necessary because of the poor retention power of human beings. The purpose of preserving written messages is to provide necessary information readily and without any delay and when it is needed. However, the following gives the main purpose of writing the messages.

- **Future references:** The limitation of the human mind and poor retention power cannot be overlooked. Written messages can be preserved as records and reference sources. Various media of communication can be filed for future reference. Thus, keeping records is essential for the continuous operation of the business.

- **Avoiding mistakes:** In transmitting messages, earlier records help in reducing mistakes and errors and also prevent the occurrence of fraud.

Legal requirements: Written communication is acceptable as a legal document. That is why some executives think that even if some messages have been transmitted orally, they should later be confirmed in writing.

Wide access: Communication media has become very fast, and written communication enjoys wide access. If the communicator and the receiver are far from each other, written communication sent through post or e-mail is the cheapest and may be the only available means of communication between them.

Effective decision-making: old documents help effective decision-making in a great way. Decision-making process becomes easier if old records are available. Because the messages provide the necessary information for decision-making purpose.

PRESENTATION

Successful presenting consists of three elements:

Content: The presentation should be packed with practical and easy-to-remember information. Inject enthusiasm about the topic into your presentation through your voice and body language. Ask the audience questions so they have to keep awake, think and answer, delegates like to give answers. Also, try to include one or two exercises to get them thinking and joining in. Keep your presentation to the point and practice it to make sure that it lasts the length of time you are allotted to speak, taking into consideration question-and-answer time if appropriate. Always remember that you may miss out on something you intended to say but the audience will never know that you missed it so don't worry about it. Tell short stories to bring your presentation to life (these may be humorous) but be careful about telling jokes as they can seem out of place.

Confidence: Remember that some people get nervous in audiences too. You can put them at their ease by showing with your body language that you are confident of your ability; let them realize they will enjoy the forthcoming presentation. Knowing that you have information to share that is valuable for others also gives you confidence and satisfaction. Confidence will come with practice and with performing and being successful.

Practice: It is extremely important to write your presentation and practice, practice, practice until you can give it with ease. It is a well-known fact that the audience will only remember 7 percent of the words you say; 93 percent of what they will remember is your attitude, tone of voice and your physical presentation skills.

Once you know your presentation thoroughly, you then have to concentrate on how to give it in the most effective and memorable way you can. Make a connection with the audience by eye contact and drawing them into the message you wish to give by making it alive and interesting. Then the audience will be listening to every word and waiting to hear what you have to say next. You can use your experiences and anecdotes to help people remember the points you are making. You can also use a mnemonic to link key messages together.

PRESS CONFERENCE

Press conference is called when an organization has something newsworthy to tell to the media, and when more in-depth approach and discussion is needed then it is possible to provide by sending out a press release. There are two major reasons for holding a news conference. One is so that a newsmaker who gets many questions from reporters can answer them all at once rather than answering dozens of phone calls. Another is so someone can try to attract news coverage for something that was not of interest to journalists before. In a news conference, one or more speakers may make a statement, which may be followed by questions from reporters. Sometimes only questioning occurs, sometimes there is a statement with no questions permitted. Press conference gives reporters a possibility to ask questions, get explanations, quotes, and photo opportunity. While organizing press conference following points should be kept in the mind:

An invitation to the conference should be sent to reporters and desk editors a week ahead of it. Closer to the date a day or two before it a phone call can be made to remind the reporters on the event.

You should organize press conference between 9-11 in morning or 4-7 in evening. Later then or before that is not good - reporters will not have time to file a story for the next day newspaper issue.

Ideally, the conference will have several persons participating: the press officer who knows the reporters will open and facilitate it. One or two prominent persons should be present, who will give a 10-min statement each on the issue (project, release, donation, opening, or similar), after which the facilitator will give floor to the reporters to ask questions. All in all, ideally it should be finished in 45 min. After that individual interviews can be given.

A "press kit" is usually distributed at a conference, containing a press release, background of organizers, report, research results, fact sheets, list of experts, etc. Sometimes even filmed material or photo material is distributed. After the conference you should send the press kit by a messenger to those media outlets that have not sent a representative at the conference.

Reporters like to say that "A press conference should scream for a headline" meaning there should be breaking news released on them. If a conference is called and there is no such news, journalists will not forget it. There is a chance that next time, even if you have breaking news, nobody will show up at the event.

Exactly because of the proliferation of press conferences, media outlets often send beginners to cover them.

If possible, media events should be organized instead of press conference. Yet, if one decides to organize a press conference, there are a number of technical details to be taken care of.

Conference

A conference is closed group discussion. A conference is usually a large gathering of persons who meet to confer on a particular theme or to exchange experience or information. A conference may be held to exchange views on some problem being faced by the organization or some other issue related to it, and it may even suggest a solution, but the suggestions from a conference are not binding. They are more in the nature of recommendations. The participants in the conference have to register for attending the conference.

Within the organization, the sales manager may hold a weekly conference of the salesmen to review sales during the week and to plan the next week's strategy on the basis of the views expressed by them. Conference may sometimes be held to give training to new employees. These employees may be exposed to a conference where necessary information about the organization is imparted to them and through discussion in an informal atmosphere, they are made to learn all about the organization, its objectives, policies, etc. This kind of conference may be described as a conference for training. Occasionally a large industrial concern may take initiative and invite delegates from other similar concerns to a conference to discuss problem of mutual interest. The host organization selects the venue of the conference, makes arrangements for the stay of the delegates, chalks out detailed program, invite eminent people to chair various sessions, selects the speakers, and at the end of the conference sends out reports to leading newspapers highlighting some of the important aspects of the conference.

AUTHOR BIOGRAPHY

Dr Zulk Shamsuddin, PhD, AMC®, CIPT, MPM®
Accredited Management Consultant®
Chartered International Professional Trainer
Master Project Manager®

Dr. Zulk is a technology and business consultant with skills and experience in learning and development, project management, design, and delivery of strategic training programs for knowledge, career development and professional skills certifications.

A certified trainer and certification counsellor of The American Academy of Project Management ® AAPM and the Global Academy of Finance and Management ® GAFM. Dr. Zulk is a senior member of the global advisory Board and the International Board of Standards.

Join Dr. Zulk international network at PMI Community

https://community.pmi.org/profile/zulkhernain

www.ingramcontent.com/pod-product-compliance
Lightning Source LLC
Chambersburg PA
CBHW071019240526
45469CB00006BD/1990